TEXAS TORNADOES

The Lone Star State's Deadliest Twisters

TEXAS TORNADOES

The Lone Star State's Deadliest Twisters

Marlene Bradford

Text copyright © 2016 by Marlene Bradford

To my husband Bill who always
encouraged me to keep writing

Acknowledgements

Librarians in many small towns throughout the state helped me locate materials from their communities and even contacted residents to speak to me. A special thanks to the librarians at Nocona and Clyde.

The librarians at the University of North Texas, the University of Texas at Dallas, and Texas A&M University provided invaluable help on newspaper collections. A special thanks to the librarians at the University of North Texas for opening the library at special times to accommodate me.

My U.S. history students at Texas A&M University brought me invaluable information, especially personal accounts of the Jarrell and Channelview tornadoes.

Edward Williams generously gave me photos of the Frost and Dallas tornadoes as well as encouragement.

A special thank you belongs to my U.S. history students at Naaman Forest High School in Garland, Texas, whose interest in tornado stories kept me motivated.

Contents

Introduction

Ask the man on the street to name something associated with Texas and the answers probably will include football, cattle, oil wells, the Alamo, the Lone Star, and the armadillo. Few will mention the weather phenomenon that plagues Texas every spring—the tornado. Yet, this ferocious storm is as much a part of Texas culture as the longhorn or the cowboy. The word "tornado," "cyclone," or "twister" is linked with Texas in everything from sports teams to music. The Texline Tornadoes, Lamesa Golden Tornado, and Memphis Cyclones play high school football every Friday night in the fall, and the Concordia University (Austin) Tornados hope to live up to their namesake by destroying their opponents in various sports. The Texas Tornado amateur hockey team, located in the Dallas suburb of Frisco, prepares players for the National Hockey League. Texas Twister Records in Duncanville produces CD's, and the Texas Tornadoes is a Tex-Mex band. Hundreds of thousands rode the Texas Cyclone and the Texas Tornado roller coasters at Six Flags Astroworld. The name Texas Twister is attached to products as diverse as nutcrackers, model rockets, and fishing rods. Even the Texas map has not escaped –the tiny town of Cyclone is eleven miles east of Temple in Bell County.

Tornadoes are not just a part of Texas culture; they are a part of the history of many towns and communities throughout the state. All 254 counties have experienced at least one tornado. More than 15,000 tornadoes have touched down somewhere within the boundaries of the Lone Star State since 1880. Most were so weak the only evidence of their brief existence was a few displaced shingles or scattered tree branches. A few, however, left behind such destruction that just a mention of them sends chills down the spines of survivors: Waco, Wichita Falls, Saragosa, Jarrell.

Texas likes to be the biggest and the best. When Alaska became a state, Texans were heartbroken—they were no longer the largest state geographically. In 1992 Texas surpassed New York as the second most populous state, a cause for celebration. Unfortunately, Texas is number one in several tornado categories: total tornadoes, number of killer tornadoes, number of significant tornadoes (F2 or above or causing a death), property losses, injuries, and deaths. Texans would gladly relinquish these honors to other states.

When spring approaches, programs to educate the public about the dangers these monsters of nature present proliferate. The governor proclaims Severe Weather Awareness Week asking schools to conduct tornado drills and emergency management agencies to practice their responses to potential disasters. The National Weather Service conducts tornado spotter training in tornado-prone counties and urges the public to purchase NOAA weather radios that provide warnings of approaching severe storms. The Texas Severe Storms Association, an organization dedicated to severe weather education, holds one of the country's largest National Storm Conferences to bring together storm spotters, meteorologists, scientists, and educators to discuss the latest information on tornado development and safety. This concerted effort to educate the public on tornado safety may be one of the reasons tornado deaths in Texas have declined in the last decade. In spite of a "population explosion," there have been forty-one deaths since 2000, and six of the last ten years have seen no fatalities.

Selecting the most significant tornadoes in a state that leads the nation in the number of these storms as well as in tornado deaths is a difficult task. I have included all individual tornadoes or outbreaks that claimed at least ten lives, were rated F5 (even if they produced no fatalities), or had unusual characteristics or historical significance. The accounts encompass more than eighty counties and several hundred towns and communities that suffered tornado strikes from 1854 through 2020. Many who read the book will be able to relate personally to at least one of the storms, either through connection to the locality or acquaintance with someone who witnessed these monsters of nature. It is my hope, however, that those who read the accounts of the horrific death tolls and devastation these monsters of nature leave behind will heed the safety measures necessary to survive if a tornado approaches their community.

Chapter 1

Tornado Characteristics

Cyclone, twister, whirlwind, tornado—the word varies in time and place—but all refer to one of nature's most destructive storms. Regardless of the name attached to the storm, it often leaves behind death and devastation.

Tornadoes are as unique as humans--no two are alike. A tornado usually appears as a white, gray, or black funnel-shaped cloud, but some tornadoes may resemble a wall of smoke rolling across the landscape. A tornado has a distinct life cycle. It is usually born as a thin funnel descending from the parent thunderstorm cloud. As it matures and expands, the rotating column of air picks up material in its path and acquires the color of the circulating debris. In its dying stage the funnel may appear as a long, thin rope. During all stages the tornado is capable of massive destruction. Most tornadoes last only a few minutes, but a few stay on the ground for up to two hours.

Some tornadoes have multiple vortices, two or more small funnel clouds orbiting a central point. The small vortices (often called suction vortices) of a multiple vortex tornado are generally responsible for the small but extreme paths of destruction. They can also explain why tornadoes supposedly "skip" houses—one house may sustain little damage while the one across the street may be destroyed.

Frequently a weather system produces numerous tornadoes in a short period of time. The definition of a tornado outbreak has varied over the decades. Dr. Greg Forbes generally defines an outbreak as "the group of tornadoes spawned by the same weather system, but that is still a little vague. I usually include in an outbreak all of the tornadoes in a contiguous-state region over a period in which there is no more than a six-hour tornado-free gap." The largest outbreak in the United States occurred on April 27-28, 2011, when 199 tornadoes killed 316 residents of five southern states. Texas is home to very few outbreaks. The largest one was a result of Hurricane Beulah when 115 weak tornadoes killed four on September 20-21, 1967.

FORMATION

As the names for the storm have changed over time, so have the theories on how tornadoes form. Several Native American tribes have legends about the creation of the tornado. Early scientists from Aristotle to Benjamin Franklin offered theories, but not until the nineteenth century did serious investigation into the cause of tornadoes begin. Most scientists in that century believed that electricity or convection played a major role in tornado formation.

By the twentieth century improvements in meteorological instruments and the growth of meteorology as a science led to more diverse theories. Some scientists suggested pressure changes or cold fronts were the necessary ingredient for tornadoes while others offered more unusual explanations such as atomic explosions or driving on the right side of the highway. Keith Browning realized that most tornadoes form inside very large, vicious storms he called supercells. Within the structure of the supercell was a special wind pattern that allowed the storms to have long lives, reach massive sizes, and occasionally produce a tornado.

Although the exact ingredients necessary for a tornado are not known, many tornadoes form in the warm, moist air ahead of a cold front. In the plains, especially Texas, tornadoes frequently occur along the dry line which separates warm, moist air to the east from hot, dry air to the west. Wind shear, or change of wind direction or increase of wind speed with height, seems to be an ingredient in many tornadoes. Tornadoes may accompany tropical storms or hurricanes that move over land, but these are usually quite weak.

LOCATION

About one-half of the world's tornadoes develop within the United States where conditions for their formation are ideal: a moisture source to the south, a cold source to the north, mountain ranges to the west, deserts to the southwest, and an active jet stream. Historically, these meteorological conditions have converged most often from Texas northward through Nebraska, an area frequently called "Tornado Alley," but in recent decades a "Dixie Alley" has seemingly developed in the states of Arkansas, Mississippi, Alabama, and Tennessee, causing great death and destruction in the South Central and Southeastern United States. More than twenty other countries, including Canada, Argentina, Australia, France, England, Italy, Germany, India, China, Bangladesh, Japan, and South Africa have tornadoes.

The 8759 tornadoes recorded in Texas from 1950 through 2020 were not distributed evenly throughout the state. Harris County (Houston) reported the most (241); Menard and Real Counties reported only two each. The Panhandle, North Texas, and the Gulf Coast counties have the most tornadoes while the Rio Grande Valley, West Texas, and the Hill Country have relatively few. For the number of tornadoes in each Texas county from 1950-2020 see appendix B.

TIME

Tornadoes strike during every month of the year in the United States, but months of peak occurrence vary by region. The prime season is March through May in the Southeast. April, May, and June are the most active months in the Midwest, the Northwest, and the southern Great Plains. The northern Great Plains, the Rocky Mountain region, and New England experience the most tornadoes June through August. The Gulf Coast states have a second tornado season in November.

In Texas, almost two-thirds of the twisters occur in the spring. May has the distinction of being the most active month while December is the least active. Tropical-related tornadoes peak in the late summer and early fall. Although tornadoes may strike at any hour of the day, the peak hours in Texas are from 3 to 7 P.M. with the most occurring about 4 P.M.

WIND SPEED

Tornadoes are nature's most violent windstorm. Only a few hurricanes have achieved wind speeds of over 150 miles per hour, but tornadic winds quite commonly exceed that speed. Because tornadic winds destroy anemometers and the possibility of a tornado passing over such an instrument is remote, indirect methods are required to determine a twister's wind speed. In 1970 Dr. Theodore Fujita devised a method of estimating tornadic wind speeds based on the destruction the storm left behind. Since 1971 the National Weather Service has assigned, when possible, a Fujita or F-scale rating to every reported tornado. In addition, the National Severe Storms Forecast Center (now the Storm Prediction Center) used photographs and damage reports to retroactively rate all tornadoes since 1950. In 2007 the National Weather Service began using the Enhanced Fujita Scale to rate tornadoes. The new scale lowers the wind speeds in each category but still relies upon destruction of structures and vegetation. The Storm Prediction website lists the 59 tornadoes that have received the F5/EF5 rating during the period 1950-2014. Since 1950, the overwhelming majority of Texas tornadoes have been F0 or F1. Only six have received the F5 rating: Waco (May 11, 1953); Wichita Falls (April 3, 1964); Lubbock (May 11, 1970); Valley Mills (May 6, 1973); Brownwood (April 19, 1976); and Jarrell (May 27, 1997).

The Enhanced Fujita Tornado Scale

FUJITA SCALE		OPERATIONALEF-SCALE	
F Number	Fastest 1/4-mile (mph)	EF Number	3 Second Gust (mph)
0	40-72	0	65-85
1	73-112	1	86-110
2	113-157	2	111-135
3	158-207	3	136-165
4	208-260	4	166-200
5	261-318	5	Over 200

(Source: Storm Prediction Center)

MOVEMENT

The average tornado moves across the landscape at speeds from thirty to fifty miles per hour, but a few twisters whirl along at speeds up to sixty miles per hour while others virtually stand still. Tornadoes can travel in any direction, but in the United States almost 80 percent of them move from southwest to northeast or west to east. Twisters do not always follow a straight line. In the dying stage many veer toward the north or south. Some follow a circular route; a few return along the path of destruction they have already left behind.

In Texas most tornadoes plow along at fifteen to thirty-five miles per hour. Spring and fall tornadoes usually travel faster than summer ones. A few tornadoes move so slowly they appear not to move at all. Near Pampa on May 19, 1982, a tornado traveled only one and one-half miles in twenty-two minutes, and the devastating Jarrell tornado of May 27, 1997, had a forward speed of less than five miles per hour. At least 75 percent of Texas tornadoes move in a southwest to northeast direction. Hurricanes that move inland along the Gulf Coast frequently produce westward or northwestward moving tornadoes.

SIZE

The majority of tornadoes cut short, narrow paths across the land. The average path width is 128 yards, and the average path length is 4.4 miles. What may be the widest tornado ever recorded in the United States (2.6 miles) occurred near El Reno, Oklahoma on May 31, 2013. The longest tornado may have been the Tri-State Tornado of 1925 which traveled 219 miles across parts of Missouri, Illinois, and Indiana. A study of tornadoes from 1950 to 1982 showed that path length and width tend to increase with wind speed. While the average F0 tornado path is 46 yards wide and 1.1 miles long, the average F5 tornado cuts a 616-yard wide and 34.2 mile long path of destruction.

In Texas the average path width is about 110 yards, and the average path length is about three and one-half miles. The widest recorded Texas tornado touched down near Gruver in Hansford County on June 9, 1971. The F-2 rated twister was over two miles wide at several different points. The longest tornado path in Texas is difficult to determine. Data banks list path lengths, but many tornadoes cross into Oklahoma, Louisiana, or Arkansas, so only part of the tornado occurs in Texas. One of the longest paths of destruction entirely within the state was the fifty-mile-long path through Wood, Camp, and Titus counties on April 9, 1919.

SOUND

Tornadoes do not come quietly. Their noise is often heard several miles away. As the storm approaches, it usually emits a peculiar high-pitched whistling sound that rapidly changes to an intense roar. Eyewitnesses most often describe a tornado's sound as like a freight train or low-flying jet airplanes.

NUMBER

Tornado statistics may be misleading. Many that touch down at night or in remote areas go unreported. Studies have suggested that only one-third to one-half of the tornadoes in the United States are counted. Nineteenth-century severe weather enthusiasts compiled lists of tornadoes covering short periods of time, but the accuracy varied from person to person and from state to state. The United States Weather Bureau began officially counting tornadoes in 1916, but it usually counted only tornadoes that caused deaths or substantial property damage; weak storms rarely appeared in the official data. To verify the effectiveness of its tornado watches, the Weather Bureau began a serious effort to count all tornadoes in 1953. The National Climatic Data Center (NCDC), the official U.S. government database for all weather events, lists 75,515 tornadoes in the United States from 1950 through 2020.

However, the NCDC counts tornadoes by county-segments; therefore, one tornado that crosses into three counties will be counted three times which leads to an inflated number of tornadoes. The most tornadoes recorded for one year was 2085 for 2011. Remember that this is counted by county segments; the actual number of tornadoes may be different—the Storm Prediction Center data base lists 1894 tornadoes in 2011. The least recorded was 201 in 1950. Because statistics for the nation and each state from these two NOAA organizations often differ greatly, use the numbers as a guideline.

Before the Weather Bureau existed, the Army Signal Corps' John Finley reported 73 tornadoes in Texas from 1853 to 1886. Tom Grazulis, a tornado statistician who established an independent database, listed 1217 significant tornadoes (those that caused a death or were rated F2 or greater) in Texas during the years 1880-1991. The NCDC recorded 9385 Texas tornadoes from 1950 through 2020. During that period the highest number of tornadoes reported for one year was 229 in 1995, and the lowest was thirteen in 1952. Regardless of which statistics one uses, Texas ranks first in the number of tornadoes, but because of its large size, it does not lead in tornadoes per square mile.

DEATHS

Almost 15,000 Americans died in tornadoes during the twentieth century. The worst single year was 1925 with 794 fatalities; the lowest yearly death toll was 15 in 1986. Tornado death statistics before the 1950s may be inaccurate though. In the nineteenth century blacks were commonly underreported as deaths. In addition, many died after the tornado from injuries the storms inflicted upon them, and there was no organization in charge of weather statistics until the mid-twentieth century. Although the numbers may not always be accurate, without doubt a tornado watch and warning system instituted in the 1950s combined with improved communications and tornado safety education has substantially decreased the loss of life from twisters in the United States.

The country's worst single tornado (although recent research revealed that this event may have been multiple tornadoes) occurred on March 18, 1925 when 695 died across Missouri, Illinois, and Indiana. A look at the list of the 20 deadliest tornadoes in the United States (see appendix A) reveals they occurred in numerous states and struck from March to June.

Texas leads the nation in tornado deaths—1815 from 1880 through 2020. During the last half of the twentieth century 538 Texans died in tornadoes. The state's deadliest year was 1953 (150 deaths). Several years had no tornado fatalities. A look at the ten deadliest tornadoes in Texas reveals that none struck the same county, but all occurred in April or May. Tornado deaths since 1950 have not been evenly distributed across the state. Only 106 of the 254 counties experienced a tornado death, and a majority of those counties recorded fewer than five deaths. The six counties that had more than 20 deaths are McLennan (114), Wichita (51), Reeves (30), Williamson (29), Lubbock (26), and Briscoe (25).

The tornado forecasting and warning system in the United States began in earnest in the 1950s. The Weather Bureau issued its first tornado forecast in March 1952, and two months later it established a separate Severe Weather Unit (the forerunner of today's Storm Prediction Center in Norman, Oklahoma). The rapid spread of television from only 9 percent of the households in 1950 to 87 percent in 1960 allowed more people to be warned of approaching tornadoes. In the same decade radar detection of tornadoes and storm spotter networks became more commonplace, especially in Texas. Sixteen Texas cities officially dedicated the Texas Radar Tornado Warning Network, at that time "the best and most up-to-date storm warning system available anywhere in the world," in 1955. The combination of tornado forecasting, spotting, and warning has substantially reduced Texas tornado deaths since the 1950s. From 1890 through 1949 Texas suffered 1192 tornado deaths. The succeeding sixty years (1950-2020) saw 573 Texans lose their lives to the deadly storms in spite of the explosion of population. The 1880 Texas population was 1.5 million; 1950 was 7.7 million; 2020 was 29.1 million.

ODDITIES

Tornadoes are capricious by nature. Virtually every twister leaves behind stories of strange occurrences such as food left untouched on the table when the entire house is gone. Many of these unusual happenings can be attributed to random chance. If enough houses are struck, the odds are in favor of a refrigerator being hurled into the top of a tree or the contents of a dresser drawer being rearranged. Some oddity reports are obviously false. No wind can defy the laws of nature by blowing a two-gallon jug inside a quart bottle without cracking either one or turning an iron teakettle inside out. Until recently, many of these unusual happenings added to the belief that tornadic winds far exceeded 300 to 400 miles per hour, but an extremely high wind speed is not needed to blow a pig into a tree top, pluck feathers from a bird, or carry a human several hundred feet. The following are some of the more unusual incidents that occurred in Texas tornadoes:

> ➢ An F4 twister rolled two full 500-barrel oil storage tanks, each weighing about 70 tons, about three miles across a field and 600 feet up the slope of a hill (Pecos County, June 1, 1990).

- ➢ A pizza deliveryman from the Flying Pizza Company was injured when he was thrown 50 feet from the ditch in which he had taken shelter (Lubbock County, May 29, 1987).
- ➢ A tornado did $40 million damage to airplanes at the Austin airport. Ironically, these planes had been moved inland to escape Hurricane Allen's winds (Travis County, August 10, 1980).
- ➢ Tragically, a tornado crossing I-27 threw a car 300 yards, killing the driver, a tornado spotter heading toward his observation position (Hale County, April 15, 1973).
- ➢ A tornado at Garrett tipped over a trailer on its first pass and flipped it upright when it retraced its path through the community (Ellis County, April 28, 1971).
- ➢ A huge tornado reportedly pushed a ¾ mile thick wall of sand ahead of it (Swisher/Hale Counties, May 31, 1968).
- ➢ The tornado that struck Ballinger carried an aluminum barbeque stand two blocks; the meat continued to cook over the hickory fire (Runnels County, April 1967).
- ➢ A tornado "shucked ten acres of corn without damaging the kernels" (Collin County, October 14, 1959).
- ➢ A playful tornado "tore screens from a farmhouse, stripped the blankets from the beds, and rumbled off, damaging nothing else" (Johnson County, June 1957).
- ➢ Another tornado carried a 5000-pound gasoline storage tank about 1.5 miles before dropping it in a lake (Briscoe County, May 15, 1957).
- ➢ Survivors of an Amarillo tornado found pigs that had escaped from an overturned truck rooting

through the remains of their homes (Potter County, May 15, 1949).

➢ A linen scarf lay untouched on a pulpit while the rest of the church lay scattered for miles (Montague County, May 18, 1946).

➢ A tornado killed one man at Ravenna (Fannin County) on April 9, 1919. His brother died a year later when a tornado struck Paris (Lamar County) on May 11, 1920.

➢ A tornado threw water 500 feet in the air when it crossed the Bosque River (Bosque County, April 23, 1908).

TORNADO SAFETY TIPS

1. **Assume every tornado is a deadly one**. Avoid staying in its path, if possible. If it isn't possible to avoid the tornado, have a place to take shelter.

2. Learn the difference between a tornado **watch** (tornado **could happen** somewhere during the time of the watch) and a tornado **warning** (a tornado **has been sighted** in your area—take the necessary precautions to protect yourself and others). Whenever a watch is issued for your area, be sure you have a way to keep up with the weather. Phone apps from television stations and various weather entities are available which will notify you in case of a tornado warning in your area. Some cities such as where I live have a reverse 911 call service to notify residents, even in the middle of the night. If possible, have a weather alert radio, especially if you live in a mobile home or in an area susceptible to night time tornadoes.

3. At home put as many walls between you and the outside as possible. This is usually a downstairs bathroom or closet, but be sure the room does not have a window or an outside wall. If your house has a basement, take shelter there. In a 2-story home a good place is often a storage area

under the stairs. I always told my students that if they had time to put on sturdy rubber-soled shoes (if your house is hit, there will be broken glass and maybe downed electric wires), to be sure they had their cell phone in their pocket, and to grab something such as a pillow, chair cushion, blanket, or even a bicycle or football helmet to cover their head. The old myth of opening windows should be ignored. Don't waste time—the first thing the winds will do is open them for you.

4. **Mobile homes are especially vulnerable to high winds**. Anyone who lives in a mobile home, whether it is tied down or not, needs to leave and seek shelter in a sturdy building. If your mobile home park has a community shelter, go there.

5. At school, follow the instructions of the principal or person in charge.

6. Ask if your workplace has a designated safe area. If not and you are in a multi-story building, the stairwell is a good place as are inside bathrooms, but stay away from windows and get downstairs as much as possible.

7. Many malls have designated tornado or safety shelter. Look for them if severe weather is a possibility on your shopping day.

8. In restaurants, grocery stores, or convenience stores walk-in coolers or refrigerators are the best places to go; bathrooms are also a possibility, but be sure they don't have windows.

9. **Cars are not a safe place to stay in a tornado**. If you are in a car and see a tornado approaching, leave your car and take shelter in a sturdy building. If you are out in the country and no building is available, get into a ditch or a culvert. Be sure to get away from your car. There are cases of people being killed by their car rolling on top of them. DO NOT GET UNDER A HIGHWAY BRIDGE OR OVERPASS—they act as wind tunnels. If you are traveling on the highway, be sure you know what county you are in

should the weather turn severe. Tornado warnings are usually issued by county.

10. If you find yourself in the open when a tornado is approaching, try to get to a building. If none is available, find a low place such as a ditch and get as flat to the ground as possible.

11. **No matter where you are, when a tornado watch is issued, think about where you would take shelter and, most importantly, KEEP INFORMED ABOUT THE WEATHER.**

Chapter 2

The Jarrell Tornado

T. S. Elliot said in his poem "Wasteland" that "April is the cruellest month," but in Texas that title belongs to May. More Texans have died in tornadoes in May than in any other month. Seven of the ten deadliest tornadoes in the state's history (Waco, Goliad, Sherman, Frost, Runge, Zephyr, and Saragosa) claimed 442 lives in May. Since 1950, four of the six tornadoes to receive an F-5 rating (including Jarrell) struck during May. Every part of the state is susceptible to these monsters; Central Texas is no exception.

On May 27, 1997, residents of Central Texas were enjoying a warm but quiet morning. School was out for the summer in most towns that dot the map between Waco and Austin. Students were looking forward to a time without school books, a time they could swim or hang out with friends when they weren't catching up on sleep. Workers went to their jobs as usual; farmers tended their crops; ranchers cared for their livestock. In other words, the day began as a routine late spring day, but it would not end in a normal manner.

In Jarrell, an unincorporated town of some 400 located on I-35 about eight miles north of Georgetown, the morning was warm and humid. Summer was fast approaching, but spring still lingered. The temperature climbed to 79 at sunrise, and a light southerly wind from the Gulf only increased the humidity. The breeze rustled the tall Blackland Prairie grass and gently swayed the mesquite and juniper trees across the rolling hills. Patches of bright orange Indian paintbrushes and white and yellow daisies dotted pastures where cattle grazed, and green leaves marked the rows of beans and corn. A driver along the interstate who took the time to look might describe the scene as idyllic, typical small town America.

At the Storm Prediction Center (SPC) in Norman, Oklahoma, the meteorologists in charge of issuing severe thunderstorm and tornado watches thought this was going to be a routine late spring day in the Great Plains. A low pressure center in Nebraska and the upper level jet stream over northern Oklahoma signaled the possibility of severe weather later in the afternoon in those areas. A weak cold front draped across Texas from the northeast corner of the state to Del Rio on the Rio Grande combined with an ill-defined low-level jet stream meant that the greatest threat in Texas would be strong winds and hail, but the weather pattern was not the typical one that would produce numerous severe thunderstorms or tornadoes. At 1:03 A.M. the SPC issued its outlook for Central Texas: "Moderate risk of severe thunderstorms for hail and damaging winds including Travis and Williamson counties." Weather balloon soundings taken throughout the morning indicated increasing instability in the atmosphere---something was up. At 10:16 the SPC issued a new convective outlook: "Conditions will be favorable for the development of scattered intense storms with very large hail...locally damaging winds and possibly isolated brief tornadoes." It did not appear that the winds were going to cooperate to produce supercell thunderstorm development or a tornado outbreak. But, Mother Nature had other ideas—she didn't follow the rules.

Shortly after noon a thunderstorm developed over southern McLennan County, and at 12:50 the National Weather Service (NWS) office in Fort Worth issued a severe thunderstorm warning for hail from a rapidly developing storm near the town of Woodway. The activity caught the attention of the SPC forecasters. Within minutes they issued a tornado watch to be in effect until 7 P.M. for much of east Texas and western Louisiana. Williamson County was on the far western edge of the watch which stated: "Tornadoes…hail to 3 ½ inches in diameter…thunderstorm wind gusts to 80 mph…and dangerous lightning are possible in this area." The National Weather Service offices in both Fort Worth and Austin/San Antonio went on high alert. They would be responsible for issuing any severe thunderstorm or tornado warnings in their jurisdictions. The war between nature and man had begun.

Lon Curtis, Bell County Assistant District Attorney and avid storm chaser, had been following the weather situation from his home in Temple thirty-five miles south of Waco since early morning. Years of experience in researching and analyzing storm data prompted him to keep a close eye on the developing storm potential. He was heading north toward the storm when he heard a Department of Public Safety dispatcher ask a trooper to check the storm for severe weather development. He decided to check for himself, and as he rounded a curve he saw across the low, rolling hills the first tornado of the day about a mile in front of him. The twister (designated the Lorena tornado later rated F2) was exhibiting two odd characteristics: it was moving very slowly and it moved from northeast to southwest. The great majority of tornadoes in the United States (some estimate that at least 90%) move from southwest to northeast, and their average speed is thirty miles per hour. This supercell was already giving notice that it was not "average," but it lasted only ten minutes, caused no injuries or deaths, and left behind $75,000 in damages.

Within minutes of the Lorena tornado's emergence from the towering thunderstorm cloud, KCEN-TV, the

NBC affiliate in Waco/Temple/Belton, broke into normal daytime programming to begin what turned out to be an eight-hour marathon. Meteorologist Bruce Thomas followed the developing severe weather and warned the people of southern McLennan and Bell Counties to take precautions to protect themselves and their families. Because very few houses in the area had basements or storm cellars, viewers were urged to go to the lowest interior room of the house, usually a bathroom or a closet, and cover their heads with pillows or blankets. Although they had learned what to do in school, fear and adrenalin take over and often cloud memory and actions. Everyone needed to be reminded that every tornado must be taken seriously---everyone is life-threatening.

A supercell, a highly-organized storm with extreme updraft winds that can produce large hail and strong tornadoes, can last for hours. This one was not going away quietly or quickly, and it wasn't following the rules—it kept heading south, paralleling Interstate 35 into Bell County. A sheriff's deputy reported a very brief touchdown at the intersection of Highway 7 and Interstate 35 in the town of Eddy at 1:44. As live pictures flashed across television screens from Waco to College Station (from where I was watching), Bruce Thomas pointed out the tornado virtually right outside the door of the station. Fortunately, the miniscule tornado (forty yards wide) dissipated after a journey of 0.2 miles. No damage was reported, but within 2 minutes a stronger tornado (later rated F3) dipped to earth in open fields southeast of Moody and moved into far northern Bell County. In its path, the twister left behind damaged property but again no deaths or injuries. The supercell was still moving slowly southward toward more populated areas of central Texas. If it held together, it could impact the northern Austin suburbs.

Now in Bell County, the severe thunderstorm seemed to say, "I'm not done yet; I'm just warming up."

The supercell, still moving slowly south-southwestward, launched another attack with an F3 tornado on the north side of Lake Belton where it destroyed 100 boats and a marina and damaged several lakeshore homes. Almost as an afterthought, the thunderstorm dropped another small, brief F0 tornado from the sky near the Stillhouse Dam in the Lampasas River Valley. Still, no injuries or deaths were reported. KCEN had adequately warned the area to be prepared for the devastation this storm could produce.

As the parent supercell crept southward, the Austin television stations sent reporters to the area of southern Bell and northern Williamson Counties to produce live shots of any tornadoes that might develop. They were not disappointed. At 3:07 the thunderstorm produced its sixth tornado about half a mile west of the Prairie Dell exit on I-35. Those traveling the busy highway stopped to observe the beautiful rope-like condensation cloud that appeared to remain stationary in a field for ten minutes before picking up speed and dancing across fields as it moved southward virtually paralleling the interstate. The F1 twister damaged trees and several structures but injured no one before it dissipated near the Bell-Williamson County line. This was the warmup for the main event.

Williamson County was no stranger to tornadoes. Thirty-nine twisters had taken two lives and injured 43 since 1950. The most serious one occurred in Jarrell on May 17, 1989, as the town slept. Clocks stopped at 4:02 A.M. when the F3 tornado cut a half-mile wide path through the town, killing one and injuring thirty-one. When the storm moved on, Jarrell discovered that twenty-five houses had been destroyed and two schools and forty-six mobile homes were damaged. The price tag was $8 million, but perhaps what was even more important for the small town, fifty people lost their jobs when eighteen businesses suffered severe damage. The community rebuilt, but the terror of that event was still fresh in their minds when storm clouds appeared on the northern horizon in May 1997.

When the mega storm crossed into Williamson County, the NWS in Fort Worth transferred responsibility to the Austin/San Antonio NWS office in New Braunfels. At 3:30 this office issued a tornado warning for Williamson County effective until 4:30 P.M. The bulletin that went to law enforcement and television stations said that "at 3:25 a tornadic thunderstorm was located about 5 miles west of Jarral (sic) moving southeast at 10 mph. This storm has had a history of producing tornadoes and large hail. The City of Jarrel (sic) is in the path of this storm." Included in the warning were the standard instructions to seek shelter: "Go to the lowest floor of your building. . . cover your head. Stay away from doors and windows. Do not stay in mobile homes or vehicles. . .get into a sturdy building." Austin and Waco television stations blared the warnings to their viewers, and in Jarrell the Volunteer Fire Department activated the warning siren. Simultaneously the SPC issued a new tornado watch for south Texas that included Williamson County.

Those who heard the eerie sound knew the possibility of a tornado or at least a severe thunderstorm hitting their town was great. In response, some jumped into vehicles and headed for interstate underpasses or sturdier buildings. Some left mobile homes for permanent houses of friends or relatives. Still others left businesses and hurried home to insure the safety of loved ones. Those who sheltered in houses followed instructions and huddled in bathrooms or closets, often with heads covered with pillows and blankets. As they waited, the storm was gathering strength, ready to hurl itself without mercy on those unfortunate to remain in its path.

The small rope tornado that touched down just northwest of Jarrell about 3:40 looked harmless. Maybe this seemingly innocuous storm would bypass the town and move into open country where it would do little damage, but the twister had other ideas. Ted S. Warren, photographer at the Williamson County bureau for the Austin American-Statesman, jumped at the chance to capture shots of the storm. Weaving through traffic as he headed north on I-35, he encountered hail and rain. Near the Jarrell exit he found crowds huddled under the overpass, looking with trepidation at the pitch black sky just north of town. He recalled thinking that he wouldn't find much destruction, maybe only a downed street sign or a barn without a roof. That was before he saw "it," bouncing and dancing its way across the open plain. "It looked like the biggest movie, on the biggest movie screen I had ever seen. For something so destructive, it almost seemed magical to watch." In just over one minute's time, this beautiful, playful cloud that mesmerized those who saw it exploded with fury into an angry, half-mile wide wedge tornado. The swirling black mass had morphed from a minimal F0 tornado into nature's most destructive wind storm, an F5 monster whose winds exceed 260 miles per hour. Some eyewitnesses reported seeing several small funnels before the tornado changed its character. A study of damage patterns after the event suggested that what looked like a single wedge tornado could have been a giant multiple vortex twister. The people of Jarrell didn't care; they knew they were in trouble.

At first the black cloud appeared to be heading toward the main part of Jarrell, a ten-block area that parallels I-35. In the path would be churches, businesses, and the town's schools. But, the rule-breaking tornado seemed to change its mind; it veered almost 90 degrees to the west, heading for the uninhabited grassland. It first touched down at Chuck Tonn's farm where it turned structures into kindling and machinery into bales of metal. Next, the twister destroyed a recycling business and several trailers on the corner of CR 305 and CR 307. Bent steel beams and snapped power poles and trees were witnesses to the storm's destructive power. Slowly edging forward at a measly five miles per hour, the indescribable winds blew vehicles through the air as easily as a fall breeze blows dead leaves. Amazingly, the angry storm ripped more than 500 feet of blacktop from CR 305, leaving only a scoured roadbed. If the core of the tornado stayed on its westward path along CR 305, it would bypass or at the worst strike a passing blow at most residences as it headed to open country. At seemingly the last second though, the tornado expanded to a width of three-quarters of a mile and made a slight jog to the southeast which put the Double Creek Estates directly in its path.

Before the storm Double Creek Estates was a subdivision of thirty-eight modest one-story brick homes built on half-acre to one acre lots. A few mobile homes dotted the area that was surrounded by small farms and pastures. Some residents had migrated from Georgetown and Austin to escape the hustle of the busier cities and to take advantage of cheaper taxes and a smaller school district. Along Double Creek Drive and Double Creek Spur families lived their lives just as those throughout the country do. They went to work and school, attended church services, and participated in community activities, never dreaming that something so horrible could in an instant end so many of their lives and forever change the lives of those who survived.

The time was 3:48. The Larry Igo home on 305, just a few hundred feet east of Double Creek Drive, was probably the first inhabited house the storm impacted. As the outer winds peeled shingles from the roof and hurled pieces of debris through fragile glass windows, the family huddled in the safest place in the house they could find, praying the storm would pass quickly. Within seconds stronger winds blew larger chunks of debris against exterior walls and lifted the roof; walls collapsed as they lost their roof support. The incredible winds sheared anchor bolts that had attached the outer walls to the foundation, leaving only vulnerable interior walls. They, too, collapsed within seconds and were blown away. All that remained of the Igo home was the foundation and small piles of rubble. The tornado had claimed its first five lives.

The roaring black cloud, churning slowly like a horrifying movie played in extremely slow motion, next attacked the homes in Double Creek Estates. Just like the Igo house, these homes succumbed to the 260+ miles per hour winds. Roofs disappeared, windows broke, outer walls disintegrated, and interior walls crumbled only to be scattered in all directions by the swirling winds. Unlike most tornadoes that move quickly through a neighborhood though, this unwanted guest remained for minutes at each place which ensured that everything would be pulverized into tiny pieces and blown away. All the homes on Double Creek Drive and Double Creek Spur suffered the same fate. Fatalities occurred at the six houses that were occupied at the time of the storm: Mullins, LaFrance, Carmona, Smith, Gower, and Taylor. But, the tornado was not finished destroying lives. After crossing Double Creek Drive, it edged across open fields toward the Keith Moehring home on CR 396. The house suffered the same fate as the others. Four members of the family along with the two Ruiz brothers who had sought shelter in their home perished. After leaving indescribable destruction in the Double Creek area, the twister again altered its course ever so slightly. It moved toward the south-southwest, crossed CR 309, and headed into a heavily wooded area of cedar trees where it dissipated.

Everyone who had seen the tornado described it in different terms. Bud Taylor had one of the more colorful descriptions: "That sky was black as night, just boiling. Like a dad-gum big bull getting ready to charge. Seemed like it set there for 10 minutes making up its mind which way to go." A young survivor said it looked like "a giant bear." The size of the monster varied from one observer to another. A man driving away from the storm in his pickup saw a black cloud "hundreds of feet across" in his rearview mirror. B. J. Barner recalled for the *Dallas Morning News*: "It was huge. It wasn't like a circle funnel, it was like a quarter-mile." In the confusion of the situation the *Austin American-Statesman* quoted one resident: "It was four miles wide and it was coming across the pasture." Regardless, those who saw the tornado did not care about its actual size. They knew it was dangerous and they had to get away.

Numbers do not do justice to the impact a tornado has on a community, but they do give an indication of the severity of the storm. The Jarrell tornado killed twenty-seven and injured twelve. Ordinarily, the number of injured far exceeds the number of fatalities, but this was no usual tornado. Baylor University meteorology professor Don Greene, who studied the Jarrell twister extensively shortly after it occurred, detailed his findings in an Associated Press article in October 1997. He explained that the Jarrell twister, which the National Weather Service rated an F5, exhibited several odd behaviors. First, this powerful tornado did not travel far, only about five miles; most F5s cover distances of at least fifty miles. Second, the tornado traveled extremely slowly. According to Dr. Greene's study, the Jarrell tornado took eleven to eighteen minutes to travel one mile through the Double Creek area which translates to about four miles per hour; the average speed of a tornado is thirty miles per hour or more. Third, the tornado traveled southwest, the opposite direction of the vast majorities of twisters in the United States. This would help to explain why it moved so slowly. Lastly, Greene concluded that the winds preceding the funnel itself were so strong they blew off the roofs and collapsed the exterior walls which left the residents "exposed to the full force of the tornado."

The Fujita scale ranks tornadoes from F0 (winds from 40 to 72 miles per hour) to F5 (winds that exceed 260 miles per hour). The National Weather Service sends a team of meteorologists and engineers to evaluate every significant tornado to determine its F scale ranking and to uncover any flaws in the warning systems that could be corrected. These men and women were accustomed to seeing the devastating impact strong winds have on structures and lives, but the Jarrell tornado astounded even the experts with its force. The storm cloud had sucked asphalt from roads, bark from trees, and hair from cattle, but even more telling was the lack of debris it left behind. "Instead of the piles of debris that mark the end of most tornadoes, houses simply disappeared, leaving only featureless foundations and bare earth." Perhaps saddest of all of the statements about the severity of the Jarrell tornado came from researchers at the Department of Geosciences at Texas Tech University in Lubbock who explained that those who cannot get out of the way of a tornado as massive and powerful as the one that struck Jarrell have virtually no options. In the words of Dr. Richard Peterson, "In the extreme case when everything can be leveled . . . if you're not in a basement, you're up a creek." This was the sad reality in Jarrell's Double Creek area.

Seconds after the winds subsided, Jarrell High School principal John Johnson emerged from one of the school's telephone booths where he had taken refuge to discover that three-foot-long strands of pasture grass from fields nowhere near the school covered his car. That's when he knew something was terribly wrong. Like others in town, he had sought shelter when several minutes earlier the warning siren that sat atop the tower at the fire station blared to notify the community of impending danger. Mr.

Johnson instinctively knew that his town was injured and perhaps some of his students were hurt.

Just as everyone who saw the monster or survived its wrath had a story to tell, each person who rushed to the aid of the small town had a tale. Residents of Double Creek who had been away when the tornado hit, flew to the site to see if they could find loved ones who might have been at home.

Aerial view of Double Creek Drive in foreground and Double Creek Spur at top of photo. Photograph by L. Phan, NIST

All that is left is the foundation. From NWS Austin/San Antonio.

Asphalt is stripped from the road. Photograph by I. Hakkarinen NOAA/NWS.

Remants of a mobile home near the Double Creek Estates subdivision. From NWSFO Austin/San Antonio.

Law enforcement from Williamson, Bell, and Travis counties as well as volunteer firefighters from several communities dropped what they were doing to rush to Jarrell to help in what they thought would be a normal search and rescue operation.

One of the first on the scene was James Blackmon, police chief and canine officer of Thrall, a small town in the eastern part of Williamson County. As he related the story in 2011 to Blake Hurtik, a journalism student at the University of Texas, one can almost hear his voice crack as he described the horror of that time. He and his deputy knew a storm was coming. They had been listening to the police scanner when the thunderstorm produced tornadoes across Bell County. Before long, they heard about Jarrell, and they knew they had to head to that town to offer what help they could provide. When they reached Round Rock, they found that state troopers had blocked the interstate heading north toward Jarrell. They, along with dozens of other law enforcement officers and troopers, found an alternate route to the stricken town. Riding with Blackmon in an old Plymouth was his canine partner; his deputy followed in the town's police car. As he traveled down CR305 toward the damage area, the car jolted like it had run off the road. He remembered thinking, "I know Jarrell is poor but this is ridiculous." The road had been paved, but the tornado had ripped away the blacktop as deep as eighteen inches. Rescuers had to inch their way through the mud and debris. When he and fellow officers reached the eastern end of what had been Double Creek Estates, they linked arms to form a human chain. Trudging through standing water and mud, they walked forward slowly looking for signs of life, but with only a few exceptions all they found were signs of death.

Blackmon, like other searchers, saw things that deeply disturbed him. He encountered what at first appeared to be a dead animal, only to discover it was the body of a deceased female. He told Hurtik that he still had a hard time talking about it more than ten years after the fact. "It was real bad. I never saw nothing like that in my life." Most of the bodies would have to be identified through forensics. As Blackmon continued along he observed that "it sandblasted everything." Buildings, livestock, cars, farm equipment, trees, even asphalt looked as though they had been through a blender. Where once houses occupied by families had stood, all that remained were bare slabs and plumbing pipes bent low by the winds. Wooden stakes protruded from telephone poles that the winds had toppled. Barbed wire the tornado had ripped from fence posts entangled bodies of dead cows.

Blackmon remembered that, after eight hours of such horror, he couldn't take it anymore. When the police chief headed away from the scene of devastation, he offered a ride to others who had reached their breaking point, too. As the old car loaded with officers holding on to the roof, trunk, and hood headed back up 305 toward town, they saw in the headlights the terrified faces of residents who could not find their loved ones. In town they passed the fire station which had been set up as a temporary morgue and the church building where people frantically searched for any information on their loved ones.

Captain Shawn Newsom of the Williamson County Sheriff's Department arrived on the scene twenty minutes after the storm left its path of destruction. He recalled "I crested over the hill and thought 'This isn't so bad because there's nothing out there.'" As soon as the thought cleared his mind though, he realized there should have been something out there but it was gone. He likened the countryside filled with only solid, flat rubble to films he had seen of the Hiroshima atomic bomb attack. Williamson County EMS Director John Sneed joined Newsom in heading up an immediate search for survivors, but they soon found there were few; the rescue part of the search would be over quickly.

In a personal letter sent to me in the fall of 1997 Allen Meissner recalled vividly that May 27. He had just gotten out of school the previous Friday and was helping his father harvest oats on their farm five miles east of Jarrell. Storm reports indicated that the supercell was heading in their direction. As the storm approached, Allen became apprehensive and called his dad on the radio to suggest they park the machines under the shed. His father said to keep cutting because the storm would soon pass, but finally the threatening clouds convinced Mr. Meissner to take his son's advice. As Allen walked to the house, he saw what he described as one of the worst sites possible, a dark funnel cloud that was "slowly creeping across the horizon from north to south." Although he was five miles away, Allen swore that, because of its size, the tornado looked less than a mile away and that at any minute it would devour a trailer on their property not far from their house. Although he had always heard it was best not to try to outrun a tornado, Allen thought that in this case the rule was wrong and convinced his dad and sister to jump into their truck and head east toward his grandmother's house in Bartlett. After the storm had passed, he called his house to see if the answering machine would respond; that would mean their house was spared any major damage. The machine did pick up, but at the same time reports of the Jarrell tornado came across the television screen. Allen and his father decided they would head to Jarrell to see "what all the fuss was about." When they reached Jarrell, they found confusion. Allen remembered that the law enforcement officers were "driving like mad looking for the damage." The Meissners followed the officers for a while, but finally gave up and turned toward home when they found nothing. It appeared that the weathermen had blown the report of a tornado all out of proportion.

A short while later, someone searching at Jarrell called the Meissner home to ask if they had any large industrial loaders or bulldozers. They said they didn't and asked why they were needed. The voice told them that there was heavy damage at Jarrell; the tornado had struck a neighborhood down in a little valley that was difficult to see from town—Double Creek Estates. The Meissners jumped into their truck and headed to Jarrell to help. As Allen phrased it, "What we saw next, I hope no other person has to ever see." In his own teenage words, he described what so many saw in a way that was real and not just for the media: "The destruction was unbelievable, for lack of a better word. Where once nice homes use to be, now nothing but dirt. Whole foundations pulled up from the ground and tossed aside. Cows were mangled and mutilated, were scattered everywhere. One of the factors of the storm that caused such gory effects was that the tornado

45

pulled up a couple miles of 6-strand barbed wire fence and sliced and ripped its victims with its force."

Everyone the media interviewed had a variation on the same words—there was nothing left. Sheriff Deputy R. B. Raby said of the subdivision "It's not there anymore. . . .It's just a flat, vacant field." Max Johnson Jr., son of the pastor of the First Baptist Church, declared "It was like a vacuum sucked everything up." B. J. Barner exclaimed "It's like someone came and just wiped it clean." Governor George W. Bush told reporters after he flew over the devastated area the next day: "It's hard to believe you're looking at a patch of earth where the life was literally sucked out of it."

Larry Hausenfluke, superintendent of Jarrell schools, huddled under the I-35 overpass as the tornado swooped down on his town. When it passed, he, like so many others who had seen the twister, ran to see what he could do to help. After a short time at the site, he returned to his office and told his secretary that the school would stay open to serve as a shelter for those who had lost their homes and as a clearing house for any aid that would come to their town. Red Cross workers hurried to Jarrell and set up an emergency shelter at the school. Late into the evening many of those whose homes had been damaged or destroyed drank coffee and ate waffles as they awaited word of what to do next. Julie Thomas, spokesperson for the Austin area Red Cross, was astonished that no one slept on the cots that lined the makeshift shelter that night. Residents who still had a home reached out to their less-fortunate neighbors to provide them with some sense of stability. Everyone stayed with family or friends.

When Wednesday dawned bright and dry, more than 150 searchers returned to the disaster site to continue to trudge through standing mud in the hopes they would find a survivor. The night before, the Austin Fire Department had brought in thermal-imagining cameras that could locate people by the body heat they emitted, and police departments brought their dogs that had been trained to sniff out bodies. Occasionally, a call would go out for a body bag—part of a victim had been found and was treated with respect. At midday Thursday the search ended—the toll stood at twenty-seven dead and twenty-seven unaccounted for.

Williamson County Justice of the Peace Jimmy Bitz had the unenviable job of supervising the documentation of the remains. Sheriff Department investigators photographed and catalogued each body before moving it to the temporary morgue at the Jarrell Volunteer Fire Department where Justice of the Peace Judy Hobbs readied the bodies for transport. At 4:30 on Wednesday morning a tractor-trailer truck left Jarrell for the short trip to the new state-of-the-art Travis County Forensic Center in Austin where the medical examiner Robert Bayardo and his team would use fingerprints, tattoos, dental records, and any other available method to match the names on the missing list to the remains.

In Jarrell families of the missing congregated at the First Baptist Church awaiting the official word of the fate of their loved ones. They hugged each other and cried as Max Johnson Sr., the church's pastor, tried to console those still reeling from the news that not only their homes but perhaps members of their family had been the victims of the horrendous storm. Some brought dental records or photos to aid in identification. Many prayed. Throughout the ordeal they often asked "why," but Rev. Johnson told reporters what he had told the people of Jarrell: "It's too complicated of a question to find an answer." On Main Street volunteers set up a table to ask survivors to put their names on a sign-in sheet to eliminate them from the list of possible dead or missing. Periodically those at the church would leave to check the lists.

As searchers continued to comb the Double Creek area, others stepped in to do what they could to help. More donors than the Scott and White Blood Center's mobile unit from Temple could handle arrived to give their blood to the injured. The Salvation Army set up their headquarters at the fire station, and the Southern Baptist Convention set up tables with food and water at the Baptist church. Boy Scouts from Taylor and Granger brought groceries to feed those in need of a meal. One Jarrell couple, Joe and Louise Hoes, had lost their home to the 1989 tornado. Friends and strangers helped them rebuild because they had no insurance. On Wednesday morning they fired up the barbeque pit at their business, Joe's Country Bar-B-Q, and cooked meat to take to the school to feed workers and survivors. They wanted to repay those who had helped them in the way they best knew how. "We will help them as much as we can, 'cause we know what it's like."

Governor George W. Bush came to Jarrell on Wednesday. He shook hands with the people at the school where his helicopter landed after an aerial tour of the destruction zone and expressed his condolences for their losses before signing a state disaster declaration for Williamson County. State Insurance Commissioner Elmer Bolton who was traveling with the governor estimated between $10 and $20 million in damages.

Not everyone in town was happy with the way officials handled the situation. Especially galling to many was the sheriff department's refusal to let the residents of the area return to check on their property. Around noon officials declared that the area was open; they believed they had found all traces of missing people. Those who were so anxious to see what the tornado had left behind were stunned. They soon realized that most of them would need only a few boxes to pack the belongings that were worth saving. Those who had hoped to find important documents,

48

family photos, and other mementos found nothing except "sheets of plastic, knots of sheet metal, pieces of vehicles, miles of twisted fence, snapshots, bills, restaurant checks, a foundation with a water heater and not much else." In most tornadoes residents who dig through piles of twisted lumber, bricks, pipes, insulation, and furniture recover a few reminders of their everyday life but not in Jarrell.

For days the media roamed throughout Jarrell looking for the best human interest stories they could find. Newspapers from small towns and big cities from New York to Los Angeles as well as all of the major television networks sent reporters. Captain Newsom recalled that one radio reporter who had no camera just walked around looking for someone to interview. Newsom told him he was too busy to talk to him, but the reporter responded: "Please give me an interview. There's nothing I can say that will describe this." His statement seemed to be the theme for several days. Even hardened veterans found it difficult to control their emotions when they heard the stories of the families who suffered so much. For nearly a week CNN had a broadcast team in Jarrell, and the major networks (NBC, CBS, and ABC) devoted segments of their nightly news casts to the town. It seemed as though everyone in America was fascinated with the story of the tiny town that had lost so much.

Each survivor had a unique story to tell the media. A very small number had survived their houses blowing apart around them. Many had left their homes to take shelter away from the tornado's path when they saw it approaching their town. Some were fortunate enough to have been away from home when the tornado barreled through their neighborhood. Most in town, however, had not suffered physical damage to themselves or their property, but they had endured the emotional trauma of seeing friends and families struggle through their losses.

The Donnie Peterson family began their morning as usual on May 27. As he headed out the door for work, his wife LaDonna urged him to be careful and to have a great day. Almost as an afterthought she added that she hoped a storm would blow through and take the heat and humidity away; at 5:30 the heaviness of the air and the heat were already oppressive. Little did she realize how prophetic her words would be.

LaDonna and her seven-year-old son Duston decided to take an early swim. They knew that by afternoon the heat would be too intense to be outdoors. Shortly before 1:00 the Storm Prediction Center issued a tornado watch for Williamson County until 7 P.M., but Mrs. Peterson was unaware of the potential danger. About 2:30 Duston turned on the television in the living room and then returned to his room. Noticing the television was still on, LaDonna randomly flipped through the channels and heard a special weather report. A tornado had touched down north of Temple. While LaDonna continued to monitor the weather on television, she had mixed feelings. She was not worried because the sky showed no evidence of an approaching storm, yet for some unexplained reason she was very uneasy. As she continued to listen to storm reports and warnings, clouds moved in from the north and the sky became overcast. Peterson did not think a tornado would strike Jarrell, but should the weather situation deteriorate she wanted her mother-in-law who lived next door to be aware of the situation. LaDonna told Duston to get his shoes and clothes on because they were going to his grandmother's for a while "just in case." When she and Duston arrived at her in-law's home, LaDonna found her sister-in-law Bonnie Hammett and daughter Bonita were also there. Kermit and Juannita Peterson's home was a substantially-built one on County Road 396 a short distance west of Double Creek Drive. Suddenly the warning sirens sounded. LaDonna rushed to the front porch and saw a "big black cloud about one mile away that stretched from the sky to the ground." Frantically she ran into the house and hollered for everyone to get into the bathroom. She put the children into the bathtub and covered them with cushions that she had grabbed from the couch, and the adults squeezed in because they thought it was the safest room in the house.

The storm did not strike immediately, but the family knew it was still there because of the pressure they felt. Anxious to see what was happening, LaDonna left the bathroom to peak out the front but saw nothing; however, when she looked out a side window, she saw a frightening sight—the tornado was stripping chunks of blacktop from the road and hurling debris everywhere. She hurried back to the shelter of the bathroom. Through the window she saw the tornado rip the roof from the barn and the donkey fly by. Suddenly, the bathroom door blew open, and LaDonna covered her head with a cushion. To keep the children calm the family all held hands and sang "Jesus Loves Me" and "Old McDonald." As the storm loomed ever nearer, LaDonna prayed "please God please don't take my family."

Wood, rocks, hay, dirt, and everything imaginable pelted the group in the bathroom, but no one was hurt. When rain began to fall, they realized the tornado had passed.

Remains of a home (Peterson) adjacent to the Double Creek Estates subdivision of Jarrell. Photograph by E. L. McIntyre, NOAA/NWS

Climbing over debris, the family emerged from their place of shelter. As rain soaked them, the Peterson family realized how lucky they were. The exterior walls and roof were gone, and everything except the bathroom was a shambles. LaDonna looked toward her house, but it wasn't there. Neither were any of the houses on Double Creek Drive. She later told reporters that "it was like a bomb had been dropped on us." When LaDonna approached the site where he home had been, she saw that everything was gone. Only broken remnants of her family's life filled the yard.

A short distance down CR 396 Virginia Davidson was mowing her lawn when she saw the tornado heading directly toward her home. She hurried into the house and huddled under a blanket in her bathtub. As the howling winds blew the house apart, they lifted her and the tub into the air and tossed them several hundred feet. "I was hanging there in the air, and all I could see was pitch black." When Virginia landed, she still had the blanket with her. Her husband James rushed home from his job in Austin to find his house destroyed and his wife missing. As he searched through the debris, he feared the worst. "I was looking for her body. I didn't expect to find her alive; not when you saw what I saw." He didn't even recognize where he was. The winds had sucked all of the fence posts out of the ground; property lines were not evident. Then, he saw a woman, bleeding and covered in mud, walking down the road toward him. It was Virginia. He took her to the hospital where they treated her only injury, a gash to her leg.

As the tornado bore down on their home on Double Creek Drive, Billy La France hurried his wife Debby and ten-year-old daughter Kristin into the bathtub. He crouched nearby on the floor. The tub wasn't big enough for all of them. They covered their heads with couch cushions. Debby recalled "I could hear things start to hit the house, tinkling sounds, it sounded like the roof was tearing off, things were tearing apart. And that's the last thing I can remember." Searchers found Debby in the branches of a peach tree near the ruins of the modest home. Kristin lay in the mud nearby, bleeding but alive. "I think this tree is what saved us, saved me and my daughter because I was in the tree and she was on the ground near it," Debby told an interviewer. She thought that if the tree had not been there, "we would have been blown on where my husband was taken and he was taken three houses down the road and he was killed."

Emma Mullins lived next door to the La France's home on Double Creek Drive. Early in the afternoon on the day of the tornado she left work at the L&M Café in Georgetown to check on her two step-grandsons, five-year-old Ryan Fillmore and his thirteen-year-old brother John Reyes, who were home alone. Just like the other houses on the fateful road, the Mullins house succumbed to the onslaught of the extreme tornadic winds. John was the only one to survive. Rescuers took him to Georgetown Hospital where confused relatives finally located him and tried to piece together the fate of the rest of his family. He told relatives from his hospital bed that he blacked out when the tornado sucked him into the air, but he remembered seeing a board pierce his grandmother and Ryan flying from the home. When he awoke, he could see that only the slab foundation remained. Doctors told remaining family members that he would not suffer permanent physical injuries, but the emotional scars would be a different matter.

The 1989 Jarrell tornado had destroyed Gabriel Hernandez's mobile home as he and his pregnant wife cowered under their bed. When he built a new home at 115 Double Creek Drive, Gabriel dug a seven-by-nine foot underground cellar to use in the event another tornado hit the area. While Gabriel was at work on Tuesday, his wife and their three children took advantage of his foresight. They survived unscathed as the most destructive part of the tornado roared overhead, obliterating any sign that a house had once stood there. Although they were trapped for half an hour because piles of debris covered the cellar door, the Hernandezes were glad to be alive. Most of their neighbors were not as fortunate. When reporters asked about his shelter, Hernandez responded: "A lot of people say that I'm the most intelligent guy in the whole neighborhood. But I think I was the most frightened. That's what saved my family."

While some survived the onslaught in their home, others chose to flee when the black cloud threatened their safety. Diane Howell and Charlie Boren, who had both worked overnight shifts, had settled in for a day's sleep in their home near the intersection of CR305 and CR307, only a short distance from Double Creek Drive. Diane had a hair appointment that afternoon. As she was closing the gate, her neighbor, Charles Bates, told her there were tornadoes on the ground near Belton, about forty miles north of Jarrell. Diane returned to the house and told Charlie about the tornadoes. He turned on the Weather Channel to monitor the situation, and she drove to a hair appointment. As she approached I-35, Diane saw a small tornado in her rearview mirror. After watching it for a few minutes, she determined it was headed for her house. About the time Charlie realized the weather situation was serious, Diane burst into the house shouting frantically "Get up! Get up! Get your clothes! Don't put them on! It's here! It's here! There's a tornado right outside headed this way!" While Diane scooped up the dog, Charlie grabbed his clothes and headed for the door where he saw the monster. He knew that they had to make a split-second decision about what to do. There would be no second chance if they chose wrongly. If Diane had not left the car doors open and the motor running, they might not have escaped to safety. Charlie ran barefooted over the gravel drive, clinging to his clothes, and hopped into the car. He described the twisting cloud closing in on them as a monster that "looked like a huge pillar, with a halo around the top, holding up the sky." About half way between their driveway and CR 307, their escape route, they saw a car fly around the corner. A pair of frantic eyes peered out of the windshield. Larry Igo was heading home to warn his wife and three children. Charlie waved for him to turn around but to no avail.

Diane headed south on the county road, away from the tornado. They, like many others that day, took shelter under the I-35 overpass. Charlie thought it was not a very good refuge, but it might save the car from hail damage. Under the bridge they heard what "sounded like many jet aircraft warming their engines before takeoff." Curiosity overcame Charlie, and he climbed the hill to the access road overlooking the valley they had just fled. A huge cloud bank, unrecognizable as a tornado, enveloped their subdivision. What appeared to be thousands of white birds circled inside the swirling cloud mass. In an instant Charlie knew those were pieces of vinyl siding from their home. Everyone who had been under the bridge was cold, wet, and shaken by the event, but they were all alive. When the Department of Public Safety released traffic, Diane and Charlie headed home. Charlie described what he saw. "We could not tell where our house had been! Everything was so disorienting! It was a mud flat!" They backed up to the corner and counted four driveway culverts. Charlie recognized a fence post and a pile of debris across the yard where a telephone pole had been. "Yep, this was it!"

Tracy Arnold watched as the twister got bigger. Inside the family-built rock-walled home near the Double Creek Estates, she prepared for the worst as she, her two children, and a niece and nephew huddled together in a closet waiting for the onslaught of the winds. Keith Bukowsky had also seen the tornado as he frantically raced his dump truck toward the house where his sister-in-law was trying to protect the children from the storm. As he pulled into the yard, the tornado was only about a thousand feet away. He screamed for everyone to get out of the house and into a car. They sped to the underpass where they watched helplessly as the tornado churned slowly along the road where their house stood. After the storm passed, they returned to find the entire house, including the closet, was gone. Arnold credited her brother-in-law with saving their lives. Bukowsky told reporters: "They say you're not supposed to run from a tornado, but I think we did the right thing."

Tonya Wagers was watching a soap opera at her home on Double Creek Drive when she looked out the window and saw the funnel. She saw the thin, narrow cloud hit the ground and spawn two other tornadoes. Not waiting to see if it would hit her house, Tonya fled in her truck.

When she came back to the site where her house had once stood, all she could find was a cage for the dog. She and her husband had survived, but her house, a van, three trucks, and five dogs were gone. So, too, were many of her neighbors on that unfortunate street.

Patrick Tucker was tired after just moving into his mother's home on CR 305 in Jarrell. After breakfast on that sunny Tuesday morning, he and his mother Kay talked briefly with neighbors in their Double Creek Estates subdivision before Patrick headed for his job in Austin. When reports of tornadoes in Jarrell came across the television, Patrick hopped in his truck and battled hurricane-force winds and driving rain as he sped northward along I-35. A police blockade at the entrance to the subdivision stopped him. When he demanded access to the area to see for himself whether his mother and her home had survived the tornado, police again refused. Nearly hysterical from fear, he bypassed the police and jumped a barbed wire fence. What he found was nothing. "I found a neighborhood that was as if it never existed. It was just razed. There wasn't even a slab to my mother's house. Everything was gone. Absolutely zero." Thinking his mother was dead, Patrick went to the high school gym that was serving as a shelter. There in a crowd of sobbing storm victims he spotted red hair like his. Tears streamed down his face when he realized that his mother was alive. She had gone to a dentist appointment and had decided not to drive home when she heard the tornado warning.

Whether they survived in their home like the Petersons, under a bridge as Diana Howell and Charles Boren, or being away from home like Kay Tucker, all would agree with LaDonna Peterson who said "we were luckier than some and not as lucky as others, but we thank God every day to be here."

All tornado deaths are tragic, but Jarrell seemed to be especially so. Of the twenty-seven who died in Jarrell, fourteen were under the age of 18. Nine families suffered two or more deaths (Carmona, Smith, Taylor, Mullins, Gower, and Mayer). All five members of the Larry Igo family perished as did the four members of the Moehring family. The Ruiz brothers left their mobile home for the more substantial home of their friends, the Moehrings, only to perish there when the house disintegrated. The boys' mother Maria died trying to reach her sons. Their mobile home was untouched.

Chapter 3

The Deadliest Texas Tornado: It's a Tie

Americans love lists. Every endeavor from sports and entertainment to education and business has a top ten list. Tornado statistician Tom Grazulis has compiled top ten lists of states for several tornado categories including total number of tornadoes, number of killer tornadoes, and total deaths. Unfortunately, Texas leads all three. The ten deadliest tornadoes in Texas history aided Texas in reaching the coveted position. These tornadoes alone accounted for 626 of the 1794 tornado deaths Texas suffered from 1880 through 2012.

#1 (TIE) Goliad (Goliad County)—*May 18, 1902*—estimated F4

Seven tornadoes touched down in northeast and central Texas before 2:00 on this late spring Sunday afternoon. One died near Detroit in Red River County, and fifteen were injured at Athens in Henderson County. The Limestone/Freestone County tornado killed three at Ben Hur and damaged thirty homes in Fairfield. These weak storms left behind minimal damage, but the day's last tornado would take its place in Texas history as the state's deadliest (along with Waco fifty-one years later).

This Sunday in Goliad was typical. The weather was nice enough for families to walk or ride in carriages to church services, but by early afternoon the wind began to gust and residents began to fear a storm was coming. Eyewitness J. W. Browne described the storm for the *Victoria Weekly Advocate*

A strong gale blew from the southeast up to 3:30 P.M. when it commenced thundering heavily in the northwest, dark clouds gathering rapidly. Large hailstorm, but scattering, commenced falling. I was sitting on the gallery of the old Fannin hotel….Suddenly a noise came like a heavy train running in the distance, it rapidly increased in power and sound until it sounded like a million ton engine running away. Everything turned to my eyes a dark brown or red color. Limbs of trees, debris and everything filled the air. God seemed nigh. A horrible roar, a sigh as the earth were dead and the rapid dum, dum dum, faster than you can think was over. I rushed to the western part of town as soon as the storm had for a moment subsided. One block west of the square—the great live oaks were uprooted; two blocks—horror! Shrieks of the wounded met the ear, the streets were litter of dead everything—people, cows dogs, cats, chickens….The dead were on every side, white and black locked in a last death clasp to what they had seized upon.

In two to three minutes the tornado had laid waste to the western part of the town of about twelve hundred residents. Beginning at the San Antonio River Bridge the twister demolished every structure along its 350-yard wide, mile-long path that ironically ended at the cemetery. The relatively small area was home to more than one quarter of Goliad's population and many of its churches. More than one hundred houses, the Methodist and Baptist churches, and the black Methodist church building were destroyed. Damage estimates were $100,000.

The loss of life was appalling. Though the official death toll is 114, many believe the count was much higher, perhaps as much as three hundred. The *Dallas Morning*

News reported thirty-eight whites and fifty-seven blacks were buried on May 19, and nine additional bodies were found that afternoon, but "there is not any reliable computation which will show the number of people killed by yesterday's cyclone." Reports circulated that at least forty died in the collapse of the black Methodist church building. Several of the injured who suffered from tetanus caused by puncture wounds died later. Entire families disappeared, leaving no one behind to identify the bodies or arrange for burial. Many black victims were buried in an unmarked mass grave at Lott Cemetery, and seven children were buried in another mass grave. A disproportionate number of the victims were children; the youngest was only twelve days old.

Goliad had no hospital or central water supply. The more than 250 injured were taken to the courthouse, which served as a hospital. Trains from Victoria, Beeville, and Cuero carrying doctors, nurses, and medical supplies arrived at the devastated town only hours after the storm. For days afterward many Texas cities and towns sent supplies, money, and workers to aid Goliad.

Newspaper accounts across the state were filled with the horrors the twister inflicted upon its victims. Some were beheaded. Telephone lines and barbed wire horribly mutilated others. One minister died when the tornado blew a plank through his torso. It was embedded so deeply the ends had to be sawed off in order to bury him. An indication of the twister's intensity is the treatment it meted the San Antonio River Bridge. The tornado picked up a huge steel beam from the twisted mass of metal, carried it two miles into town, and "hurled it into the ground near the county courthouse like a giant spear." It remains as a reminder of one of the state's two deadliest tornadoes.

#1 (TIE) Waco (McLennan County)—*May 11, 1953---F5*

Most Texas cities have been a victim of tornadoes, but only once have two cities suffered major death and destruction on the same day—May 11, 1953. At 9:30 that morning the New Orleans Weather Bureau office issued a tornado forecast for an area of Texas bounded by San Angelo, Waco, Wichita Falls, and Big Spring. Shortly after noon an F4 tornado devastated San Angelo, leaving behind thirteen dead and millions of dollars in damage (see account in next chapter).

In Waco C. A. Anderson at the Waco Weather Bureau Office learned of the San Angelo disaster but he did not wish to alarm citizens of his area unnecessarily. Anderson told the Waco Times Herald that there was no cause to worry in Central Texas because no tornadoes had developed in the area yet. Besides, all Waco residents knew that according to Huaco Indian legend a rim of hills surrounding their town on the banks of the Brazos River ensured its protection from tornadoes. Some citizens were aware of the tornado forecast, but most went about their daily routine, paying little attention to the weather. Roger Conger, an employee at a Waco gas station, was on duty when his wife telephoned him to ask whether he had heard the tornado alert on the radio. His attitude was the common one of the day: he laughed and told her that he had not heard the forecast, but it would not make any difference because Waco had never had a tornado. Many residents, especially those who did not own a television or had not been listening to the radio, were unaware of the tornado forecast, but some who had survived tornadoes in other parts of the state or country sensed something was ominous about the clouds that approached the city from the southwest.

About 4:10 P.M. a funnel cloud dipped to earth three miles north of Lorena in McLennan County and moved northeastward through the community of Hewitt. In Waco rain fell in sheets, and hailstones as large as three inches in diameter pelted sections of town. Downtown many sought refuge in buildings or cars parked along the main thoroughfares of the city of eighty-five thousand residents. Shortly after 4:30 the wedge-shaped funnel roared through the business district. Buildings crumbled burying hundreds of people, many in passing or parked cars. Two square miles of the downtown area were devastated. Electric power and telephone lines were down, creating traffic nightmares and disabling communications systems. Hardest hit was the block bounded by Austin and Franklin avenues and Fourth and Fifth streets. Fifty-six died in this block alone. Most deaths were a result of the crumbling of older structures such as the Dennis and Padgitt buildings; seventeen died in the rubble of the Torrance Recreation Hall alone.   Thirty-eight more perished in the square around City Hall and nine died in automobiles. Eerily, the twenty-two story Amicable Building soared virtually unscathed above the utter devastation. When it was built in 1911, the founder of the life insurance company had ordered the building to be constructed to "withstand any type of punishment, including tornadoes." The building swayed in the tornadic winds but did not fall thanks largely to the more than four million pounds of steel and iron that went into its frame.

Numbers alone cannot adequately describe the devastation. The final death toll was 114 which gave the city on the Brazos the distinction of tying with Goliad for the greatest number of deaths from a single tornado in Texas history. More than one thousand survived their injuries. Nearly 2000 automobiles were damaged or demolished, 850 homes suffered some type of damage, and more than 500 other buildings were either destroyed or deemed unsafe for occupancy. The price tag for the tornado was a staggering $51 million. Ironically, a meteorology graduate student at the Agricultural and Mechanical College of Texas (now Texas A&M University) in College Station about ninety miles south of Waco was observing the college's radar on the afternoon of May 11. Don Moore was studying the application of radar to weather forecasting when he noticed an unusual, quickly moving cloud formation on the radar screen. Photos taken at 4:32 P.M. showed five large radar echoes, but no one at the college paid particular attention to the comma-shaped echo until they heard the news of the Waco disaster. When the meteorology faculty studied the radar photographs, they realized the Waco tornado had been evident on the screen. Had they known what the echo represented (this was before it was commonly accepted that hook-echoes frequently represented tornadoes), they might have been able to warn the city of the approaching tornado.

*Destruction in downtown Waco. From Texas
Collection at Baylor University*

*Another view of destruction in downtown Waco.
From Texas Collection at Baylor University*

Chapter 4

Rounding Out the Top Ten

#3 Rock Springs (Edwards County)—
April 12, 1927—estimated F5

Rock Springs, a town of about eight hundred residents located on one of the highest points of the Edwards Plateau, was an oasis in the thinly-settled semiarid ranching country. Although the railroad did not run through the county seat of Edwards County, Rock Springs survived as a center for wool and mohair production. Beautiful scenery and bubbling springs attracted tourists, but tornadoes were not frequent visitors. No significant tornado had ever struck the county, so residents were not concerned when the sky darkened and a northeasterly wind began blowing in the early evening of April 12. They expected, at the most, a spring rainstorm, but a mile-wide tornado struck the unprepared town at 7:50. Observers from miles away saw a red cloud over the town, and those in Rock Springs who were looking to the north saw a cloud dip to the ground near the town. The two-inch hail that was falling did not mask the grinding noise that accompanied the violent twister. Within one and one-half minutes most of the town's buildings disappeared, even the foundations.

In the darkness dazed survivors crawled from beneath splintered houses and the crumbled stone walls of business establishments. Help from the outside would not come immediately; communications were severed when the tornado destroyed the telephone exchange. Telephone operator Gladys Lowery and a lineman drove over a mile to the nearest unbroken line. From there she relayed the news of the storm by a telephone nailed to a post. From Uvalde, about seventy miles to the southeast of Rock Springs, forty cars filled with doctors, nurses, and relief workers set out to help the stricken town. Medical personnel from San Antonio endured a harrowing night of travel over muddy roads and flooded creeks before they reached Rock Springs early Wednesday morning. Army troops from Fort Clark brought blankets and tents for the homeless and patrolled the town. The First State Bank minus its windows served as a morgue, and the Edwards County Wool and Mohair Company building became a temporary hospital. The most seriously injured were transported by ambulance to Camp Wood and placed on a train to San Antonio.

When daylight arrived, townspeople began to assess the physical damage. The town's only two churches and the school were demolished, the courthouse was without a roof, and every house was destroyed. Only twelve of the town's four hundred buildings stood, but they were only shells. Losses would exceed $1.2 million. Lieutenant Luther Smith, who flew over the town the morning after the tornado, described the devastation: "Rocksprings looked to me as if some giant hand had scattered matches over the ground. There was nothing standing intact. The frame houses were piled up like matches and splinters. The brick and rock buildings also were torn about."

The devastation the tornado visited upon the buildings was horrific, but it could not compare with the loss of life the town suffered. At least seventy-two died, and more than two hundred were injured. The death toll would have been much higher if physicians had not administered tetanus shots to all the injured. Ed Tracy, a volunteer who cooked for the townspeople and rescue workers, wrote in his memoirs that he saw twenty dead young women laid out in the street. Among the dead were the editor of the *Edwards County Leader* and the Methodist minister and his wife.

Wholesale burials occurred on Wednesday afternoon. No church building stood, no resident minister was available, and the town had no undertaker. Volunteers undertook the depressing task. They prepared the bodies, and in many cases the victims were buried wearing the same clothes they had on when the storm struck. Local carpenters built coffins, and some additional ones arrived from Kerrville. Soldiers dynamited crevices in the rocks of the town's small cemetery to provide graves. Survivors placed makeshift markers on the graves where family members were buried together.

After the storm, survivors related accounts of their ordeals. Delfine Fuentes was nursing her six-month-old baby when the tornado struck. A falling timber killed the child she was cradling in her arms, but she survived. Joe Cordova threw a rope around his wife and his four siblings and tied it to a post rooted in the dirt floor of the home where they had taken shelter. The house flew away, but the family remained firmly anchored to the post. When his house blew away with the first winds, high school Principal Seth Young tried to shield his wife from the orange-sized hailstones that beat down upon them. The wind blew the couple apart, and Mrs. Young ran for shelter in the new brick school building. She was seriously injured when the storm turned that structure into a pile of debris. C. A. Harrington desperately held the door of his home closed against the wind. When he looked around, the rest of the house and his wife and five children were gone. As he frantically searched through the debris, he stumbled upon the porch of a neighbor's home that had escaped complete destruction. He fell unconscious inside the front door—in the midst of his family. The winds had hurled Mrs.

Harrington and the children across the road, and only one child sustained injuries.

Destruction in Rock Springs. From author's personal collection.

#4 Sherman (Grayson County)--*May 15, 1896--estimated F5*

All spring the weather had been unusually dry and abnormally warm. On May 8 the first rain of any consequence in two months fell on Grayson County. During the next seven days high humidity, hot days, cool nights, and falling barometric pressure created the ideal conditions for severe weather. About 1 P.M. clouds began to appear southwest of Sherman. Shortly afterward, a tornado killed two and injured twenty-five in Denton County. At Justin the storm damaged twenty-two homes and every business in town. Thirty minutes later another Denton County tornado killed three people and destroyed seven homes in Gribble Springs.

In Sherman the afternoon had been unusually dark. The wind blew from the south and southeast then died away completely; the air became sultry and oppressive.

Several layers of clouds moved slowly in different directions. About four o'clock a thunderstorm with small hail and rapidly shifting winds drenched the town. At Pilot Point, about twenty miles southwest of Sherman, a tornado touched down then widened to four hundred yards as it moved northeastward through farm homes west of Farmington and Howe. Six people died including a mother and her two children who refused to go to the storm cellar with the family they were visiting.

The rotating black cloud kept on its northeastward journey directly toward Sherman. As it neared town, a few heard a roar, but they thought it was freight trains or electric cars rumbling along the stony streets. Most were in their homes or businesses and heard nothing. The tornado swept over Cemetery Hill then fortunately turned toward the north and northwest, sparing much of the town. The storm left a path of destruction two miles long and from sixty to four hundred yards wide through the west side. Fifty homes were destroyed; twenty of them were completely gone. Fifty-six died outright, and ten more died later from their injuries. Seventeen families endured multiple deaths. Many victims were not found until the next day. They had been blown several hundred feet from where their homes had stood. Damage estimates were $200,000.

Fortunately, the majority of Sherman's citizens escaped the horror of the winds. In the minutes following the catastrophe they gazed in awe at the destruction. Only piles of rubble remained where a few minutes before homes filed with families stood on tree-lines streets. The cries of the injured mixed with the wails of those whose loved ones were dead. After the initial shock, the people of Sherman rushed to aid the injured and search for the missing. Every spare vehicle in town was requisitioned to transport the dead to morgues set up in vacant warehouses around the courthouse square. The number of injured was more than the small hospital could handle. Many received care in private homes. Several students from the North Texas Female College volunteered as nurses. They thanked God that the tornado had veered westward when it was just two blocks from their school, sparing their campus and the nearby Mary Nash College (another private female college). More than four hundred young women had escaped injury.The day after the tornado the barometric pressure fell to 29.10 inches and ominous black clouds, reminiscent of the previous day, scooted across the sky, but no whirling funnel dropped to earth. The prostrate city went about the business of searching for survivors and burying the dead.

Nineteenth-century tornadoes were not rated, but the utter destruction this one left behind would have earned it an F-5 rating. The twister tore apart the iron structure of the Houston Street Bridge, twisted it into unrecognizable shapes, and hurled it into the creek below. Shingles and other pieces of the lives of Sherman residents rained down upon Denison ten miles to the north. A trunk top with the owner's name on it was found in Indian Territory (now Oklahoma) more than thirty-five miles from Sherman. Numerous descriptions of freak occurrences accompanied the Sherman tornado. H.L. Piner's account of the tornado, *Sherman's Black Friday,* describes a few of these strange happenings:

Six cans of concentrated lye were sitting in a row. A splinter was driven through the center of all, tying them all together....A horse with a close haltar on his head was tied in a barn. The barn was taken, sills and all, and even the haltar (that you could not have removed without unbuckling) was gone, and the horse stood in his unhoused stall without a scratch upon him . . . . At Mrs. Browns' house, bermuda grass was taken up as if done by a gardener spade, while flowers in the same yard were untouched. A small garden hoe was hanging on a post five feet from the residence. The house was taken and the hoe was left just as it hung before the storm.

Two views of the Houston Street bridge after the Sherman tornado.

#5 Glazier (Hemphill County); Higgins (Lipscomb County)—*April 19, 1947--estimated F5*

When Texas Panhandle residents awoke on April 19, they did not suspect that this day would be the deadliest in history for their area of the state. They knew that April storms were more likely to be blizzards than tornadoes, and the official forecast called for only showers and thunderstorms with mild temperatures. By late afternoon a giant thunderstorm cloud formed near Amarillo. At 5:42 a narrow tornado dropped from its base and followed the Santa Fe Railroad tracks northeastward toward White Deer. As nine crewmen held on for dear life, the twister derailed a twenty-one-car freight train, injuring two of the men. Nearby a few dozen construction workers atop an eight-story grain elevator scrambled down a ladder when they saw the storm approaching, but they were spared when it changed direction. The tornado struck one house on the edge of White Deer then lifted, but this small twister was only the forerunner of one of the nation's deadliest tornadoes.

Gathering strength from the warm, moist air, the massive parent storm cloud produced a multiple-vortex tornado with winds exceeding 250 miles per hour. Fortunately, the monster dodged the towns of Pampa, Miami, and Canadian, but it did not spare Glazier, a community of 150 in Hemphill County. In about one minute the tornado, by now at least a mile wide, wiped the town from the face of the earth. All that remained were the tiny concrete jail and the bank vault. An accurate death toll was hard to determine because no one knew the exact number of men stationed in the area with railroad and highway construction crews, but the accepted number for Glazier is seventeen.

Next in the tornado's path was Higgins, a town of 750 near the Oklahoma border; it suffered a fate similar to Glazier's. Some residents saw what appeared to be balls of fire before they heard the intense roar of the one and one-half-mile-wide tornado. All of the descriptions of the horrors tornadoes inflict on human beings applied to Higgins. Devastation was incredibly extensive; it was hard to imagine that a town had ever stood on the site. Only six buildings had any semblance of a wall left. Piles of brick and mortar filled streets and sidewalks; boxcars lay on their sides. An overturned heating stove ignited a fire that smoldered for hours in the ruins of the business district. Fifty-one died, and 232 suffered injury. The town physician and a nurse rendered first aid to the injured by the light of candles and torches until help arrived from surrounding towns. Thomas McCurdy, the airport manager at Canadian, and his twelve-year-old son Bill watched the tornado and described it as "five or six small twisters circling the main column." For two days after the tornado McCurdy flew his plane repeatedly to Glazier and Higgins to ferry the injured to the Canadian hospital; tangles of barbed wire and telephone lines made the roads impassable. The injured filled the high school gym and basements of the Baptist and Methodist churches at Canadian when the hospital ran out of room.

In such times of confusion, bizarre tales that often prove untrue circulate. The editor of the *Pampa Daily News* reported that at Glazier, "the intensity of the winds was evidence by the fact the bodies of two persons, together when the storm hit, were found almost three miles apart." Another report circulated that an elderly woman was found with a sixteen-penny nail in her forehead and her eyeballs plucked out.

After leaving two Texas Panhandle towns in utter ruin, the storm continued its northeastward journey into Oklahoma where it killed at least 107 at Woodward. Later studies showed that a family of tornadoes was responsible for the 170-mile long track of death and destruction that began in Texas and ended in Kansas. The day's toll was staggering: 181 killed, nearly 1000 injured, and more than $7.5 million in damages ($1.5 million in Texas).

Only house left standing in Glazier. From NWS Amarillo.

Complete devastation at Glazier. From NOAA.

#6 Wichita Falls (Wichita County); Vernon (Wilbarger County)—*April 10, 1979---* F4

Early in the day severe weather forecasters knew that tornadoes would threaten the Red River Valley of Oklahoma and Texas, but nothing appeared unusual to the residents of the area on the Tuesday before Easter. Just before 2:00 the National Severe Storms Forecast Center issued a tornado watch for north central Texas. Wichita Falls radio and television stations passed the information to the public, and storm spotters hurried to their designated observation posts. This routine is common in Texas during the spring. Very often no tornadoes form, but this was not the case on 10 April. Three F2 and two F4 tornadoes roared through parts of six counties, leaving behind fifty-four dead, over eighteen hundred injured, and approximately $500 million in damages.

One resident said, "When you live in Wichita Falls, it's not IF you'll be hit by a tornado, but WHEN." Indians who once lived in the area said it was foolish to build a town where so many fierce storms struck. History had shown that both were probably right. Wichita Falls had experienced two tornadoes before Black Tuesday. A small twister damaged three hundred homes in the north part of the city on April 2, 1958, and the 1964 F5 tornado killed seven.

The deadly tornado did not sneak up on Wichita Falls. Local television and radio stations began broadcasting tornado warnings about five o'clock. The city's siren system sounded for the third time that day at 5:50, just before storm spotters reported a large tornado was approaching Memorial Stadium on the southwestern edge of town. Despite the advanced notice of impending danger, many residents either did not hear the warnings or did not know what to do to save their lives. Forty-two died, and 1740 were injured when the F4 tornado, at times 1.5 miles wide, slammed through residential and shopping areas in the southern part of the city of nearly one hundred thousand residents.

The center of destruction was the Faith Village area that looked like ground zero in an atomic blast. When the tornado approached Sike Senter Shopping Mall, a voice on the loud speaker warned about a thousand shoppers to take cover. Most ran for a sunken garden and escaped injury when the twister sucked out skylights and windows. Along the tornado's path apartment buildings, mobile homes, frame and brick houses, businesses, and schools all suffered the same fate—they were turned into piles of rubble. More than three thousand homes, one thousand apartment units, and one hundred businesses were damaged beyond repair. Fortunately, Midwestern University students were on spring break; the university suffered only minor damage.

Homes destroyed in the 1979 Wichita Falls tornado.
From Texas Collection at Baylor University.

Virtually every person who survived the tornado had a story to relate. A husband and wife who operated an ice cream parlor in the mall crawled into the ice cream vault. An assistant manager at a supermarket who saw the tornado approaching herded customers and employees into the walk-in cooler. At the National Guard Armory sixty guardsmen who were preparing to leave for tornado-stricken Vernon crouched in a storeroom while the tornado flattened the building. Many Wichita Falls residents survived by huddling under mattresses and in bathtubs and closets, but several who tried to outrun the storm in their cars died. The Wichita Falls tornado is unique—the majority of the deaths occurred in vehicles. Ironically, many of the twenty-five who died in automobiles were fleeing homes that the tornado never touched. The city of 100,000 was without electricity and phone service, and rescuers struggled to find those trapped under the rubble. Help came from the city's neighbor, Sheppard Air Force

Base. The base opened its medical facilities, provided traffic control and property protection, and offered every type of aid from food and shelter to heavy equipment.

Those familiar with tornado ratings wonder why this monstrous tornado is not rated an F5. The answer is simple: Dr. Fujita personally rated the April 10 tornadoes, and in his judgment, an F4-level tornado produced the worst damage. Regardless of the rating, the losses were staggering: 42 dead, 1740 injured, more than 20,000 homeless. The $400 million damage estimates placed the Wichita Falls tornado among the costliest up to that time.

#7 Frost (Navarro County)—*May 6, 1930—estimated F4*

Culture and 275 miles separated Navarro and Karnes counties, but a common fate united the two areas of Texas on May 6, 1930, when devastating tornadoes roared across sections of Central and South Texas. Statistics would record this as one of the deadliest days in Texas tornado history: 81 dead, 268 injured, and numerous communities altered forever. Strong winds raked most of the state throughout the day. Tornadoes killed one on the east edge of San Antonio, one near Ottine in Gonzales County, and a husband and wife near Bronson in Sabine County. Communities from Abilene to Gonzales and from Spur to Marshall reported extensive damage and injuries, but as destructive as the windstorms were, they were minor compared to the death and devastation the two major tornadoes would leave behind.

In mid-afternoon a tornado formed near Abbott and traveled northeastward through Hill County. Sixteen died on farms near Bynum, Irene, and Mertens. Advanced warning kept the death toll to twenty-two at Frost, a town of nearly one thousand residents in Navarro County about twenty miles west of Corsicana. Townspeople heard the tornado's roar and watched in horror as the black cloud that appeared to be in two sections "bounced" toward the town. Sam Gerber described the approach of the storm: "It looked like a long plume of smoke approaching form the southwest. It hung for a moment over a small lake, and then was on us with a burst of fury."

Mrs. W. A. Ivy, wife of the town barber, pulled passersby and neighbors into her storm cellar when she saw the black cloud approaching. First National Bank president J. C. Beck rushed employees into the bank vault; none were injured. Frost jailer F. E. Dickinson filled the brick city jail with women and children then held the door closed against the wind's onslaught. Mr. McCary who owned the butcher shop hid with some friends in the store's walk-in refrigerator. At the town's school, students huddled under their desks when they saw the storm approaching. Superintendent Harrison ordered students to hurry downstairs and crouch against the wall on the lower floor of the school building only seconds before the tornado tore away the building's roof. No students were injured. Ironically, when League Wooley saw the storm approaching, he drove quickly to the school and took his daughter home. Mrs. Wooley and the child died in the wreckage of their home, and he sustained serious injuries. Near Frost two school teachers, Lois Rogers and Millie Yarbrough, knew the seventy-five children in their care faced certain injury or even death if they remained in the frame school building. The women herded their charges into a cotton field and instructed them to lie flat along the rows. From their safe vantage point they watched in horror as the tornado demolished the school. Dozens of people unable to reach storm cellars or basements in time lay in ditches to escape the storm's fury. Very few people were on the street when the tornado struck; all of the dead were buried beneath collapsed buildings. Three men, including the owner, died when Patterson's Drug Store caught fire.

The F4 tornado virtually destroyed Frost. The jail was the only public building left standing. Most of the white victims were taken to hospitals in Corsicana and Hillsboro while the bodies of the black fatalities were wrapped in blankets and placed in a wrecked building that had been cleared of debris. No house of worship survived; services for the victims were conducted in a private home. Even the community cemetery suffered when the storm overturned tombstones and monuments. Damage estimates in Central Texas exceeded $2 million.

Aerial view of Frost. From author's collection courtesy of Ed Williams.

Destruction at Frost. From author's collection courtesy of Ed Williams.

#8 Runge (Karnes County) and Nordheim (Dewitt County)—*May 6, 1930*—estimated F4

Around five o'clock in the afternoon the day's second F4 tornado left a twenty-mile long trail of death and destruction across rural Karnes and Dewitt counties. Most of the thirty-six deaths were on farms and ranches south of Runge and Nordheim where families of Mexican farm laborers lived in flimsy tenant houses. One of the greatest tragedies occurred on the L. G. Duderstadt farm near Stanley; nine members of the Zaragosa Garcia family perished. Their bodies were found more than 300 yards from the hilltop where their home had stood. Only the father, who had been in the fields when the storm struck, survived. The four Duderstadt children were unharmed in their house a short distance from the Garcia home.

Three miles south of Runge a mother, four of her children, and two other relatives died in a house on Mrs. C.F. Grosse's farm. Nearby on the J.W. Deborah farm a mother and three of her children were killed when the tornado left their home and all of the farm buildings in rubble. The father and three other children were seriously injured. Near Nordheim the tornado lifted Emil Huck's home from its foundation and blew it against his son-in-law's house. Huck's daughter died instantly, and the others were severely injured. The twisting winds scattered remnants of both houses for one-half mile. Thousands of dollars' worth of stock on the Huck farm perished. Heavy rain and hail made the search for victims difficult. Farmers who had escaped the tornado rode houses to house on horseback, checking on their neighbors. The dead and injured were transported through flooded fields and roads in wagons to the nearest town where stores served as morgues and hospitals. Damage estimates in South Texas were about $125,000.

#9 Zephyr (Brown County)—*May 30, 1909*—estimated F4

At least thirty-four people died and seventy received injuries when what the *Austin Statesman* called "the most terrific of any cyclone ever seen in this section" cut a narrow path through a residential area of Zephyr shortly after midnight. The day had been warm and oppressive. Several residents later reported a sense of foreboding and apprehension throughout the day. When thunderstorms formed west of town after sunset, many residents sensed they would be spending part of the night in their storm cellars, but they breathed sighs of relief and went to bed when the storms passed north of town. About midnight a narrow funnel cloud dropped to earth a few miles west of town. Many who saw the approaching tornado reported the black rolling cloud threw out "balls of fire" as it plowed into the town of about five hundred people with a tremendous roar.

About fifty houses, six businesses, two church buildings, and the high school were destroyed. Lightning struck a lumberyard, starting a fire that destroyed an entire block of businesses. The townspeople were too busy rescuing survivors from the wreckage to worry about fighting the fire. A section hand on the Santa Fe Railroad rode a handcar to Brownwood to get help. Within two hours the railroad sent a special train carrying nine doctors and many Brownwood citizens to aid the stricken town. They arrived to find the hillside covered with dead animals and humans. Newspapers of the day did not spare the gory details. The *Statesman* reported that "a hog, roaming the debris-strewn streets, was killed while attempting to devour the body of an infant," and that "bodies were found twisted about trees and in every conceivable shape." Supposedly, two children were blown more than two miles from the town.

Every deadly tornado leaves behind survivors with incredible stories. Mrs. Oscar Ware, who lost her husband and four children in the tornado, recalled that she and her family were running to a neighbor's storm cellar when the tornado struck.

I knew that I was up in the air, was conscious most all the time. Sometimes I would fall to the ground, and one time I fell on my face and thought I would lay there, but just as that thought came to me I was up in the air going again. Sometimes was on my head, and again on my feet, and then on my back or side; and while flying was cut very badly. One ear was almost cut-off by wire; a nail in a plank struck in my hand, I pulled it out while flying in the air.

The floor of the J. B. Arnold house plowed a ditch about 10 inches deep and 150 feet long when the winds picked up one of its corners and carried it across the street. None of the twelve people in the house was injured although eleven of them ended up in one pile. The other, Arnold's son, had remained on his cot as it made the journey across the street. One rescuer related the sad story of a husband, injured in the storm, who frantically sought his wife. He found her seriously wounded, but she would survive. The husband, however, would succumb to injuries he did not realize he had suffered.

#10 Saragosa (Reeves County)--*May 22, 1987*--F4

Tornadoes are not common west of the Pecos River. Reeves County had reported only twenty tornadoes from 1950 through 1986, and the county had suffered no tornado fatalities since records began in 1916. When dark clouds formed on the northern horizon in mid-afternoon, residents of the small Hispanic agricultural community of Saragosa paid little attention. In spite of the muggy May weather and thunderstorms in other parts of the county, the evening would be one of celebration. Graduation ceremonies for the Head Start children from Saragosa and the neighboring town of Balmorhea would be held at the old Roman Catholic Church building that served as the Saragosa Community Center.

A severe thunderstorm watch was in effect when about eighty people filtered into the frame and concrete block structure. While the children performed their program, clouds churned overhead. At 7:54 P.M. the Midland National Weather Service Office issued a tornado warning for south central Reeves County (the Saragosa area). Several funnel clouds formed and dissipated before a thin tornado touched down about one mile southwest of Saragosa near Interstate 10. As it moved toward the community, the twister strengthened into a large, multiple vortex tornado. In the path of the violent one-half mile wide tornado lay the residential and business section of Saragosa and, sadly, the community center. The four-and five-year olds were finishing their poems and songs when

Javier Lozano ran into the building warning the crowd that a tornado was coming. Javier escaped in his automobile with his son, but his wife, who could not hear him in the noisy crowd, stayed behind. Frantically, parents grabbed children and shoved them under tables and benches or flung themselves on top of the little ones. Many held hands and stood along an outside wall. Within a minute the storm struck. Twenty-two perished in the hall when the steel-reinforced concrete wall caved in on those who had taken shelter against its base. Sixteen were visitors or relatives from other towns.

Many Saragosa residents who did not attend the ceremony heard the warnings on television or saw the tornado approaching when they checked on the threatening weather. Although they knew what precautions to take, their community had no storm shelters or substantial buildings where they could seek safety. Four died in mobile homes, three perished in a frame home, and one died in an automobile while trying to outrun the tornado.

Throughout the night volunteers from all the major towns within a 150-mile radius of Saragosa streamed into the crumbled community. Rescue squads, ambulance crews, and law enforcement officers struggled to rescue the injured and retrieve the bodies of the dead. Ordinary citizens brought equipment to move the heavy concrete blocks and cut through steel rebar in an effort to rescue those trapped in the collapse of the community center. Others from miles away brought food, water, portable lights, and generators. It seemed to the survivors of the disaster that all of West Texas came to the rescue of a community that few outside of Reeves County had ever heard about.

Joel Muniz and Martin Garcia, two high school students who had been watching the approaching storm from their neighboring front yards, gave their account of the tornado's formation. Martin described two smooth clouds, one light gray and one very dark that collided "like two rams running head-on and smashing their heads." Joel added that "as they collided, they began spinning, like a Spanish girl doing a wild dance." The young men agreed that the tornado had seemed to make a U-turn right over the town. Like many tornadoes the Saragosa monster left behind unexplainable oddities. Two religious statues stood untouched in the midst of the devastated Our Lady of Guadalupe Church. At the site of a flattened home stood a wooden table; on the table sat an intact, unfrosted birthday cake.

The F4 tornado had cut a three-mile long path through the heart of the community, destroying seventy percent of the town; only a few buildings on the extreme east and west edges of town escaped with minor damage. In addition to claiming 30 lives, the tornado injured 121. Damage estimates were $8 million.

Chapter 5

Other Deadly Texas Tornadoes before 1950

Without question, tornadoes have swarmed over the area from the Red River to the Rio Grande for centuries, but accounts of tornadoes in Texas before 1880 are very rare. Most early books on Texas history fail to mention these storms. Occasionally, a local history will include tales of storms, but because of confusion in terminology, it is sometimes difficult to determine whether these storms were tornadoes or violent thunderstorms. Newspapers reported scenes of death and destruction, but they were often unclear about the type of storm. In his book *Tornadoes* John Park Finley, the country's first tornado expert, reported 102 Texas tornadoes from 1853 to 1886, but he gave no dates or locations for any of the tornadoes, so his statistics are difficult to verify. One difficulty with earlier sources is the death count. Before the 1950s the number of fatalities among members of minority groups were frequently undercounted. In addition, final death tolls were often set only one or two days after the tornado when many were still critically injured. Frequently, some of these people died, but the death count was never amended.

May 28, 1880: **Savoy (Fannin County)**

Shortly after 10 P.M. Savoy merchant W. S. Adair thought ten-pound hailstones were hitting his house, but when he looked out the door, he saw through the lightning flashes that the "hailstones" were fragments of demolished buildings flying through the air. When the wind subsided, Adair found the tornado had cut a 250-yard wide path through the Fannin County town of about three hundred, destroying every business and twenty-five homes. Fourteen of the town's residents died, and sixty suffered injury. The Savoy College building, one of the few left standing in town, was converted into a temporary hospital. Not until the next morning did a relief train from Sherman, Denison, and Bonham bringing doctors and supplies reach the stricken community. Debris from the town was found forty miles away.

April 28, 1893: Cisco (Eastland County)

Under cover of darkness, a half-mile-wide twister roared toward Cisco where many of the nearly three thousand residents were in bed, unaware of the approaching danger. Within two minutes Texas's worst tornado to the time devastated the town, leaving behind 23 dead and about 150 injured. Only a few houses and one business building remained standing. The winds overturned the twenty-ton engine and blew several cars of one train more than fifty feet then pushed another freight train which had its brakes set more than one and one-half miles down the track.

In the aftermath, citizens from throughout the state sent workers, relief supplies, and money to aid the stricken town. Newspapers estimated damage at $2 million, but a more likely figure is about $400,000. The death toll may have been higher because many people were critically injured when the final count of twenty-three was set.

March 17-18, 1894: Emory (Rains County); Hallsville (Harrison County)

From 5 P.M. to 1:15 the next morning eight tornadoes skipped across east Texas. Thirteen died and eighty-seven suffered injuries. About 7:20 P.M. a tornado "shaped like an hour-glass, forked at the bottom" moved through the west side of Emory in Rains County, leaving behind four dead, fifty injured, and $25,000 in property damage. West of Hallsville in Harrison County, the last of the tornadoes demolished a farmhouse in which thirteen people were sleeping; eight died. The body of one infant was found in the treetops.

July 5, 1905: **Montague County**

The county's deadliest tornado killed eighteen and injured forty when it wiped out the small farming communities of Barrel Springs, Long Branch, and Dixie. The death toll would have been much higher if most residents had not taken shelter in storm cellars. Deaths occurred in nine different homes. The Samuel Tumbleson family of the Barrel Springs community suffered six deaths. Mr. Tumbleson and a son, working in the field at the time the tornado struck their home, held tree branches over their head to keep the hail from beating them to death. In Montague the storm blew off the dome of the courthouse and leveled the Methodist and Christian churches.

April 26, 1906: **Bellevue (Clay County)**

Late in the afternoon, heavy rain and small hail fell on the Clay County town of Bellevue. As many of the town's five hundred residents watched in horror, a funnel cloud dropped to earth about a mile west of town. When they realized the tornado was heading their way, most ran to take shelter in storm cellars. Within a few minutes, the violent storm destroyed the entire town with the exception of the railroad water tower and a few homes. Every person who took shelter escaped, but seventeen who did not perished, including a mother and five of her children. One man, who just before the storm had told a friend that God would take care of him, was found in the rubble with a wooden spike through his heart.

May 25, 1907: **Llano, Van Zandt, and Rains Counties**

Three strong tornadoes swept across parts of central and east Texas on the afternoon of May 25. Rain had been falling for several hours when a tornado blew a Llano County farmhouse into "kindling." Three members of a family died. The terrible hailstorm that followed on the heels of the tornado killed chickens and cattle and stripped limbs from trees.

Farther to the east, another tornado cut through the east side of Wills Point in Van Zandt County, leaving behind three dead, twelve injured, and $50,000 damage. This was the third time in twenty years that a tornado had struck the town. Locals claimed that all of the twisters had formed on the same small tract of land about a mile south of Wills Point.

The deadliest tornado of the day visited Emory about 6:45, killing six and injuring forty-five. At points along its path, the twister uprooted three-foot-in-diameter trees, demolished fifty homes, and plucked chickens clean. Downed wires prevented news of the disaster from immediately reaching the outside world, but a later report in the *Dallas Morning News* called the storm "unquestionably the most destructive that has ever occurred in the State"(reports of the Goliad tornado had not been widely circulated).

June 10, 1909: **Leuders (Jones County); Haskell (Haskell County)**

Two tornadoes swept through small farming communities near Abilene during the late evening June 10. About 8 P.M. one twister cut a ten-mile long path through rural sections of Jones County two miles northwest of Leuders. The "Swedish community" suffered four deaths (all members of the E. Gilrup family), ten injuries, and the loss of sixty head of cattle and horses. At least fifty houses were destroyed or damaged.

About two hours later a smaller tornado killed six some three miles east of Haskell. As the tornado approached, most residents sought shelter in the storm cellars. Mrs. R.S. Middleton, four of her six children, and a young cousin who was visiting perished at the Middleton place when the storm blew the house on top of the cellar, crushing the roof and burying the dead beneath the rubble. Mr. Middleton and two children, who were standing on the cellar steps, escaped death. They ran immediately for help, but it arrived too late. The following day a severe windstorm accompanied by hail and torrential rain damaged a majority of the buildings in Haskell itself.

April 8-9, 1919: **Collin, Grayson, Fannin, Henderson, Van Zandt, Wood, Camp, Titus, Bowie counties**

Seven deadly tornadoes pounded ten counties north and east of Dallas in the nighttime hours of 8-9 April 1919. One cluster of three tornadoes that roared across parts of Collin, Grayson, and Fannin counties around midnight killed 27 and injured more than 130. The counties' larger towns were spared, but many small farming communities clustered around the Grayson/Fannin border suffered terrible destruction. One died at Delba, six at Blue Ridge, three at Ector, eight at Ravenna, two at Canaan, and seven at Mulberry.

At Canaan near Sherman one of the tornadoes destroyed sixteen houses, a cotton gin, a church, a school building, and a cotton warehouse. The twister overturned all but five cars of thirty-two-car Katy freight train and blew many of them twenty to sixty feet from the track. At Ector two brothers were killed when they stopped to put on clothes before joining their mother and brother in the storm cellar. One body was found a quarter mile from where the house had stood. The six deaths at Blue Ridge were all members of the Lawrence family. At another house a pocketbook with $300 was hidden between the mattresses. The tornado blew the mattress from a bed and scattered $20 bills around the property. After the storm, the home's owner found one of the bills stuffed in a coal oil can's spout. The tornado that struck Mulberry followed the road to the Red River and leveled every building in its path. Extensive damage occurred at Leonard and Trenton; several were injured, but no lives were lost. About three hours after the Grayson/Fannin tornadoes, a violent tornado killed twenty in Henderson and Van Zandt counties. Among the dead were a father and his four children who died when their home was destroyed near Canton. Another family near Grand Saline lost three members.

Another tornado carved a fifty-mile path of destruction through Wood, Camp, and Titus counties. Hardest hit was Wood County—twenty died and seventy-five were injured. Three people, including the mayor's niece, died near Mineola. Homes literally vanished in the Spring Hill, Concord, Oak Grove, and Stoup communities. Property damage in the county was $150,000. Four members of one family died west of Mt. Pleasant (Titus County). The same day two other tornadoes in Bowie County killed six and injure twenty-seven, and a renegade tornado, not part of the above storm system, injured one and left behind $100,000 damage at Mullin in Mills County.

In every county touched by the tornadoes' wrath hundreds of heads of livestock died and thousands of dollars of crops were destroyed. With electric wires littering the countryside and railroads paralyzed, communication was difficult. Perhaps the most appropriate description of the devastation was this headline in the *Sherman Courier*: "Angel of Destruction Passes over Texas."

April 13, 1921: **Melissa (Collin County)**

A deadly tornado formed near Franklin and headed toward Melissa, a town of about one thousand, shortly after two on a Wednesday afternoon. Many people were in the stores, and students filled the school building. The tornado demolished every business in town except the bank, destroyed all the town's churches, and heavily damaged the school building. Eleven lost their lives and eighty were injured, but the toll would have been much higher if many had not run for storm cellars when they saw the twister approaching.

When Superintendent G. C. Hester saw the tornado bearing down on his school, he ordered the 240 pupils and 5 teachers downstairs. Although the tornado swept away the entire roof and collapsed second-floor walls, no one in the building was killed or seriously injured. Before the storm, the two-story Waldon Hotel faced south. Afterward, the frame building faced west and rested directly against the school building.

Many residents of McKinney saw the funnel cloud, and when news reached their town that a tornado had devastated Melissa, doctors and other relief personnel rushed to give aid. Because all electric lines to the town were down, rescuers worked through the night by the light of lanterns or fires the storm had started. The same day a tornado at Petty (Lamar County) killed one child, and another tornado in Liberty County killed a man when it rolled the truck in which he was riding.

April 8, 1922: **Rowena (Runnels County); Oplin (Callahan County)**

Shortly after midnight the first of eight significant tornadoes to strike eleven counties formed near Rowena (Runnels County). The Crossroads Schoolhouse community about six miles northwest of Rowena suffered the brunt of this tornado, the deadliest of the outbreak. Seven died and fifty-two were injured. The same tornado killed five and injured twenty near Oplin in Callahan County when it blew apart several small homes.

One died when a small tornado damaged or destroyed fifty homes and an oil refinery in the western part of Electra in Wichita County. Near Cleburne (Johnson County) a man died when another tornado destroyed the barn in which he had sought shelter. The two tornadoes that struck Stephens County claimed no lives but demolished highway bridges, more than thirty oil derricks, and half the buildings in the village of Crystal Falls. Another tornado damaged thirty homes and demolished the Katy freight depot in Cisco (Eastland County). Other counties that suffered tornado damage were Coleman, Young, Brown, Grayson, and Fannin.

May 4, 1922: **Austin (Travis County)**

Twin tornadoes that formed over the capital city about 5 minutes apart in late afternoon carved parallel paths of destruction. Twelve died and more than fifty suffered injuries when the twisters moved southward about 3 miles apart. The "western cloud" whirled through the State School for Negro Deaf, Dumb, and Blind then destroyed several camps at Deep Eddy along the Colorado River. Five persons were injured at the school where "a little deaf negro boy, was caught by the tornado as he ran to the big campus bell to ring it and sound the alarm. He was rolled over and over for a distance over 300 feet, regained his feet and ran pluckily, back toward the bell which he finally reached."

The "eastern cloud" did most of the damage and took all of the lives as it plowed a 15-mile track from just southeast of the Capitol to Manchaca. In its path was St. Edwards College which endured more than $200,000 damage. One student died when the storm demolished a dormitory. One priest told reporters the students of the college were ordered to lay flat on the ground when the first notice of the approaching storm came. One youngster, whom the priests of the college could not reach in time with their warning, was standing upright, when the wind stripped him of every stitch of clothing, but left him unhurt. Absolutely nude, the boy wandered into the main building and coolly told what had happened to him without apparently realizing the destructive effect of the tornado.

Two deaths occurred in homes in the Penn Field area, seven died at Oak Hill, and two died near Manchaca. The St. Elmo community was virtually wiped out. Near St. Elmo two boys hurrying to shelter stopped suddenly when a wagon and two horses fell from the sky right in front of them; the horses were uninjured. Damage estimates from both tornadoes totaled over $500,000.

May 14, 1923: **rural Howard and Mitchell counties**

What may be the strongest tornado ever to strike West Texas carved a crescent-shaped path of destruction up to one and one-half miles wide across some of the most heavily populated parts of Mitchell County. The funnel first touched down about five miles southeast of Big Spring (Howard County), passed just south of Colorado, and just missed Lorraine before it dissipated. Twenty-three died and 250 were injured as prosperous ranch houses that dotted the rolling West Texas plain were reduced to splinters. The storm struck between 4 and 5 A.M. without warning. Fortunately, many ranch families, accustomed to waking early, were already doing morning chores and had ample time to get to storm cellars.

Newspapers reported several oddities. A three-month-old baby was found alive in a field but no one knew who or where his parents were. An eighteen-year-old girl blown half a mile escaped unhurt. One family's house was flew threw the air a considerable distance and came to land in the next field. All of the family members were unhurt, and the house was intact with even the mirrors unbroken.

The Southwestern Telephone and Telegraph Company reported that a large number of its poles just disappeared. Texas and Pacific Railroad crossties were blown so far they could not be found. A newspaper photographer who visited the spot four miles south of Colorado where a large ranch house had stood found nothing except the earth to photograph.

May 9, 1927: **Nevada (Collin County); Garland (Dallas County)**

Three deadly tornadoes plowed across North Texas in the early morning hours of May 9, leaving behind 40 dead and 160 injured. Hardest hit were Nevada in Collin County and Garland in Dallas County.

About 2:30 A.M. a powerful tornado that swooped down on the sleeping town of Nevada killed sixteen and wounded seventy-five. The town's citizens did not have time to take shelter—the tornado formed just outside town. About three-fourths of the town was destroyed; losses were $650,000. Survivors struggled through darkness to rescue those trapped in debris. The Baptist Church became the morgue and the hospital. As the Nevada tornado dissipated, another one formed just to the east in Hunt County. This storm killed a couple near Celeste and four people in one home near Wolfe City. Damage estimates were $150,000.

Remains of Nevada Bank. From author's collection.

The morning's third tornado targeted a residential section of Garland, a town of fifteen hundred located fifteen miles northeast of Dallas. Five members of the C.O. Smiley family along with six of their neighbors perished when the storm struck at 3:10 as residents along Austin and State Streets slept. Forty residents of the town suffered injuries. Debris was carried more than ten miles. Whims of the storm were in evidence everywhere: cars were left unmarked when garages were removed from around them; eggs were left unbroken in the midst of piles of debris; some dead chickens had all of their feathers while others had no feathers or even no heads. A family of five escaped injury when they "rode with their house as it was lifted in the air, hurtled directly across the street and deposited on

99

the lot it formerly faced." The house landed on a cow, killing the creature. Damages exceeded $100,000. One reminder of the tornado is the town's library system named for former businessman S. E. Nicholson who died in the storm along with his mother.

Damage in a Garland neighborhood. From author's personal collection.

March 30, 1933: **San Augustine, Shelby, Angelina, Nacogdoches, Smith Counties**

Five tornadoes wreaked havoc across seven East Texas counties on the afternoon of March 30. About 3 P.M. a narrow tornado traveled twenty miles across parts of

San Augustine and Shelby counties. Most of the damage occurred near Shelbyville and Neuville. Two people died in tenant homes. Among the injured in Shelby County were a teacher and several pupils trapped in their collapsed schoolhouse at the Calvary settlement. The *Dallas Morning News* reported on April 1 that the teacher and one student died, but other sources do not mention these deaths. (See note in beginning of chapter about counting deaths)

The deadliest tornado of the day claimed thirteen lives as it meandered thirty-three miles through the piney woods. At Odell, two miles from Huntington (Angelina County), five died. The Huntington drug store became an emergency hospital. Etoile, a lumbering village southeast of Nacogdoches, virtually disappeared; two deaths occurred. Six more died across Nacogdoches and San Augustine counties when the storm slammed into farm houses and logging camps. Another tornado killed two in Smith County. No deaths occurred in twisters that touched down in Houston and Van Zandt counties.

February *8, 1935*: **Murray Plantation (Houston County)**

A small, weak tornado that destroyed plantation tenant houses in the Trinity River area of Leon and Houston counties killed twelve and injured seventy. One death occurred in Leon County, and the remainder occurred on the Murray Plantation near Grapeland (Houston County). A. E. Murray gave the following description of the horror unleashed upon his 4600-acre cotton plantation:

My wife, four children and myself were eating supper when we heard the roar of the wind. The house rocked. I jumped from the table, grabbed our 6-months-old baby and then we all rushed to the east room. Within a few seconds the crash occurred. I heard my negro farmhands screaming, pigs squealing and from the noise I judged that my mules and cows stampeded, but I never dared to move. Soon I heard the roof of my house being ripped away. I gathered my wife and children closer to me. I thought it was the end. Finally the terrific wind died out enough for me to venture out. I will always remember what I saw. My 31 tenant houses were completely wiped of [sic] the earth's face. I raced the few hundred yards from my house to where the tenant houses once stood. Half-way there I started stumbling over dead bodies and the injured. As I crawled through a barb–wire fence I saw a negro cut in half. It was apparent the tornado had picked him up, tossed him into the sharp fence and simply sawed his body into half. Another negro was lodged high in a pine tree begging for help. He died before we could get him down.

June 10, 1938: **Clyde (Callahan County)**

A violent tornado (retroactively assigned an F-5 rating) formed about eight miles north of Clyde around 7:30 P.M. The clearly-visible funnel, described as "a vast column of brown earth sitting in a big brown bowl," moved so slowly toward the town, most residents had time to escape. Three members of one family, trying to reach shelter at a neighbor's house, died when the twister tore their car apart. Two hours after the storm Bell Telephone linemen found the family's two small children in a ditch about half a mile from the car. The older boy was struggling to keep his three-month-old brother's head above water. The storm destroyed twenty-one homes, many of them in one subdivision that literally vanished. Fourteen died including the town's school principal. Doctors from Baird and Abilene rushed quickly to aid the small town, and a National Guard unit from Abilene helped local officials keep order. They were needed the following weekend when over fifty thousand sightseers jammed the town.

April 28, 1942: **Crowell (Foard County)**

A fourteen-year old boy who drove to Vernon for help told the Wilbarger County sheriff that "everything in Crowell was torn up and a lot of people were hurt." Law enforcement personnel and volunteers from surrounding counties who rushed to the Foard County seat found the town of nineteen hundred in ruins. The courthouse was in shambles, and church buildings and businesses were piles of brick and timbers. One block of businesses was smoldering ruins; no water or equipment was available to fight the fire the tornado caused. Entire blocks of residential areas "just vanished." Sixteen hundred townspeople were homeless. No utilities were working, so doctors and nurses labored through the night in the beams of automobile headlights. The storm (retroactively rated an F4) killed 11 and injured 250.

One of the most publicized stories of the tornado's bizarre behavior involved the courthouse clock that stopped at 8:40. It appeared undamaged, but when officials climbed into the tower to see if they restart the clock, they found that only the dial hands remained—the mechanism had vanished.

January 4, 1946: **Nacogdoches (Nacogdoches County); Palestine (Anderson County)**

In the early afternoon a tornado derailed the last three cars of a freight train about five miles south of Decatur (Wise County); five railroad workers were injured. From 8:30 to 9 P.M. four more tornadoes danced across East Texas, killing 28, injuring 327, and leaving behind nearly $2.5 million in damages.

At Clawson (Angelina County) a half-mile wide tornado took three lives and destroyed forty-eight homes. The thunderstorm generated a new tornado southwest of Nacogdoches. This violent tornado (retroactively assigned

103

an F4 rating) killed 6, ripped apart 80 homes, and damaged more than 450 other buildings on the west side of Nacogdoches then claimed three more lives northeast of Allenby. Several thousand acres of forest were flattened.

About nine o'clock a small tornado injured seventeen and destroyed eleven homes at Peniel (Hunt County). At the same hour the day's deadliest tornado was sweeping through Anderson County. Hardest hit communities were Southview, two miles south of downtown Palestine, and nearby Livelyville on the Rusk Highway. Fifteen died and more than sixty were injured. Downed power lines made the search for victims difficult. At Southview rescue workers used a loud speaker truck to direct search efforts.

As usual, many who escaped with their lives had stories to relate. When Livelyville resident Mrs. J. H. Hightower heard a noise that sounded like a train, she instinctively thought of a tornado. Only a few weeks before she had read a magazine article about a mother who saved her children from a tornado by shoving them in a closet. Mrs. Hightower yelled for her husband and four children to hide in a closet. She and the three children who reached the closet escaped injury, but her husband and other child, who were a little slow to react, were injured. The house was wrecked, but a bowl of eggs with not a shell cracked remained on the kitchen table.

Chapter 6

Deadliest Tornadoes since 1950

March 13, 1953: **Knox City (Knox County)—F4**

Friday the thirteenth was unlucky for residents of northwest Haskell County and southwest Knox County. A violent tornado that hop-scotched eighteen miles across the area killed seventeen and injured sixty. In Haskell County a mother and four children died in their home near Jud; four others died near Rochester, and three were killed near O'Brien. A gentle rain was falling on Knox City when the twister roared into the east side of the town of about two thousand inhabitants around 2:30 P.M. About 150 homes were damaged or destroyed in an eight-block area. Hard hit was the Knox County Hospital; all the windows were shattered and the roof was blown off. The twenty-seven patients escaped serious injury but had to be transported to surrounding towns for further care. Five residents of Knox City died including a retired rural mail carrier and two visitors to the town.

May 11, 1953: **San Angelo (Tom Green County)---F4**

Most Texas cities have been a victim of tornadoes, but only once have two cities suffered major death and destruction on the same day—May 11, 1953. That morning the New Orleans Weather Bureau office issued a tornado forecast for an area of Texas bounded by San Angelo, Waco, Wichita Falls, and Big Spring. Shortly after noon a rural observer notified the state highway patrol that he had sighted a funnel cloud near Sterling city about forty miles northwest of San Angelo. Patrolmen tracked the tornado southeastward (not the usual direction tornadoes travel) toward San Angelo, a city of fifty-two thousand. Fortunately, the tornado moved slowly enough to allow the highway patrol to warn residents. The advanced warning saved lives.

Directly in the tornado's path on the northern edge of San Angelo was the Lake View area. At the Lake View School one thousand elementary and high school students and their teachers huddled in hallways just as they had during tornado drills. The twister removed the school's roof and crumbled its walls, but no students lost their lives; twelve suffered injury, none serious. One seventh grader described the terror the students faced:

"I knew something was going to happen, but I didn't know what. There was a frightening rush of wind. Glass, dust, dirt, sticks—everything seemed to crash into the room and the hall....Then the roof was either sucked off or blew off....The rain came down on us and we huddled together screaming and crying...but you couldn't hear the crying and screaming for the wind and rain." For ten minutes the tornado plowed a path one-half mile wide and 3 miles long through the Lake View residential area, leaving behind 13 dead, 159 injured, and 1700 homeless. More than 500 homes, 19 businesses, and 150 automobiles were heavily damaged or destroyed. Damages exceeded $3 million.

April 2, 1957: **Dallas (Dallas County)---F3**

Everyone saw it. Clear skies below the dark, tornado-producing cloud made the twister that plowed across parts of Dallas visible for miles. The light conditions, time of day (4:15 P.M.), and closeness to downtown attracted hundreds of photographers who took thousands of photographs and shot hundreds of feet of film. The funnel's slow movement allowed radio stations to broadcast live reports and television cameras to follow the storms' movement through south and west Dallas. A week after the tornado WFAA-TV produced a thirty-minute documentary "Disaster Dallas." All of this activity earned this tornado the distinction as one of the most photographed and studied in history.

The funnel first touched down at Cedar Hill about 4:15 and began a meandering sixteen-mile northward path through Oak Cliff, the West Commerce Street Industrial District, the Trinity River bottom, and across Harry Hines Boulevard to near Love Field. After more than thirty minutes on the ground, the tornado dissipated just north of Bachman Lake. The final totals were 10 dead, 216 injured, and more than $4 million in damages including 125 homes and 6 apartment houses demolished. The death toll could have been much worse. Personnel breathed a sigh of relief when the tornado veered away from Parkland Hospital that for the next several hours would be the main treatment center for the city's tornado victims.

The same afternoon six other tornadoes raked the north Texas area. Three weak twisters injured six in Collin and Grayson counties about the same time the Dallas tornado was on the ground. Shortly before the Dallas storm a tornado in Montague County injured one woman who escaped serious injury by hiding under her bed. One man died when a tornado cut a path from near Ben Franklin (Delta County) to west of Paris (Lamar County); fortunately, the towns had been warned. The final tornado of the outbreak destroyed building and injured one in Wise County.

Tornado over Dallas. From author's collection courtesy of Ed Williams.

Damage in a Dallas neighborhood. From author's collection courtesy of Ed Williams..

May 15, 1957: **Silverton (Briscoe County)---F4**

Thunderstorm clouds had been in evidence all day. That evening two tornadoes did minimal damage to a few homes in the Vigo Park area about 8:30. A third tornado about 10 o'clock killed a woman near Lone Star before lifting into the clouds about twelve miles southwest of Silverton. Intense lightning and menacing clouds sent some Silverton residents to storm cellars. Others turned on the television to check the weather report on the late news, but at 10:35 the electricity went off, silencing televisions and allowing listeners to hear the dreaded roar of an approaching tornado. The terrifying force cut a three-block-wide and eight-block-long path of destruction through a residential area of the town of about 850 people. Those in its path had only seconds to take shelter under beds or in closets. Twenty died, and eighty were injured. Seven

109

members of one family died when their homes, located next to each other, were scoured to the foundations. At another home the parents and three children died. More than sixty houses were damaged or destroyed. Damage estimates were over $750,000.

Strange occurrences were abundant in the Silverton tornado. The front end of a car was found in the middle of a field; the rest was found two hundred feet away. The twister picked up a car, tossed it one hundred feet into a loaded grain truck, and blew both vehicles into a ditch. It also carried a five thousand pound gasoline storage tank about one and one-half miles and dropped it into a lake.

April 17-18, 1970: **twelve Panhandle and South Plains counties**

Six significant tornadoes pummeled twelve Panhandle and South Plains counties from 9 P.M. to 1 A.M. Twenty-three died, and 141 were injured. The night's first tornado heavily damaged homes and school buildings in the small towns of Whiteface (Cochran County) and Whitharral (Hockley County). Twenty-four were injured, but no deaths occurred. Fortunately, players and spectators at the Whitharral school gym had taken shelter only minutes before the F4 tornado flattened the building.

About ten minutes after the first tornado struck west of Lubbock, a second twister or possibly two on the ground at the same time ravaged areas north of Lubbock. Near Cotton Center (Hale County) the storm killed a woman and her son in their pickup truck. Moving northeast, the tornado struck the southwest edge of Plainview and traveled at rooftop levels through the business district, leaving behind smashed plate glass windows, damaged automobiles and roofs, and tree limbs in the streets. In the Seth Ward community on the northeast side of town the F4 tornado leveled almost everything in its path. Plainview reported no deaths, forty injuries, and $4.5 million in property damages. The twister continued northeast on its fifty-five-mile long path, killing two near Claytonville (Swisher County) and one at Silverton (Briscoe County) where it moved two fifty-foot tall grain storage tanks a quarter mile.

A third F4 tornado near Lazbuddie (Parmer County) destroyed three farm homes and left one dead. Two weaker tornadoes injured two near Hedley (Donley County) and ten at Pampa (Gray County).

About an hour after midnight the night's deadliest tornado touched down in rural Swisher County where it damaged homes and killed cattle. Northwest of Clarendon the twister claimed a life in a rural home then headed for Sherwood Shores, a retirement village and resort on Greenbelt Lake. Most residents, many of them elderly, were asleep when the tornado blew more than 150 trailer homes apart. An *Amarillo Globe-News* reporter on the scene described the utter destruction: "The frame of one trailer was found two miles away. The tornado even pulled the grass out of the ground. Bodies were scattered amid the debris. The survivors were in shock." Before dissipating near McLean, the tornado killed a couple in rural Donley County and blew several tank cars off the railroad tracks. Debris from this F4 twister fell on Wheeler County, several miles to the east.

May 11, 1970: **Lubbock (Lubbock County)---F5**

The 5 P.M. forecast for Lubbock mentioned only the possibility of rain, but by sunset thunderstorm clouds towered to over forty-six thousand feet. About eight o'clock the Lubbock Weather Bureau office received reports from its Amarillo counterpart, which had more sophisticated radar, that the storm clouds reached an incredible fifty-five thousand feet. Forecasters in the South

Plains knew that such cloud heights signaled severe hail and often tornadoes. A few minutes later golf-ball size hail began to fall three miles south of the city of 170,000 that had escaped a serious tornado threat for more than seventy years. Shortly thereafter, an off-duty policeman reported to the Weather Bureau that he had spotted a funnel cloud seven miles south of the airport. Based on this report and radar echoes, the Bureau issued a tornado warning for Lubbock County. The city's radio and television stations broadcast the warnings, and many residents took precautionary actions. The city and surrounding area received a pounding from the hail, but no tornado touched down.

Shortly after 9 P.M. radar indicated a tornado on the city's east side. While emergency personnel focused their attention on this threat, at 9:35 a funnel dropped from the greenish clouds directly over the city. Touching down first just east of the Texas Tech University campus, the tornado, at times up to one and one-half miles wide, roared into the downtown area and continued northeastward through warehouse and residential areas before lifting near the Weather Bureau office at the municipal airport. The tornado's eight-mile long journey through the city left behind incredible destruction. The twenty-five-square-mile devastated area represented more than one-fourth of the city. More than 600 apartment units, 430 houses, and 250 businesses were destroyed; more than 10,000 automobiles and 119 aircraft suffered severe damage. Even worse, twenty-fix people lost their lives and more than fifteen hundred were injured. A conservative damage estimate of $135 million made this one of the costliest single tornadoes in U. S. history. Ironically, the Lubbock storm occurred on the seventeenth anniversary of the Waco tornado.

Many citizens had little notice of the impending disaster. Civil defense sirens sounded only briefly before the noise of the storm drowned them out and the ferocious winds destroyed the power lines that operated them. The one Spanish-language radio station had already signed off the air. Others were caught in cars when the storm struck. Emergency communications were disrupted when the tornado struck the City Hall. An announcer on the city's emergency broadcast radio station, located in the *Avalanche-Journal* building, shouted into the microphone "Take cover" as the twister struck the newspaper office.

One of the hardest hit areas was downtown. The tornado's winds ripped marble and concrete slabs from the sides of buildings, tossing them onto parked cars below, and shattered more than eighty percent of the windows. Upper floors of the twenty-one-story Great Plains Life Building, the tallest structure in town, swayed as windows popped. The tornado deformed the building's steel structure (the word "twist" was never used in published reports), causing it to be abandoned for several years.

From downtown the tornado cut a path through commercial warehouses before turning its fury on a Latino neighborhood where few structures offered any protection from the storm. Ten died in this area as houses collapsed on them. Three motorists died in their vehicles at the intersection of Loop 289 and U. S. Highway 87, and the tornado destroyed several motels and businesses in the area. Along Mesa Road northwest of Highway 87, the devastation was incredible. Veteran reporters and military men described the scene as similar to that in Europe after the massive bombing raids of World War II. Some families escaped death in storm cellars or closets, but others were no so fortunate. One entire family consisting of a father, mother, and two pre-school children perished when the tornado flattened their new brick home, leaving behind only the concrete steps and front porch. Nearby, a father died when the tornado hurled the entire family into a field.

Barry Carlile, a senior at Lubbock High School, was working at the Bonanza Steak House on Broadway in downtown Lubbock. When the electricity went out at the restaurant, the boss sent everyone home. On his drive home Barry saw destruction that the tornado had left behind, but he was not prepared for the sight of his neighborhood. As he neared home, he could see that some houses looked fine but others had been severely damaged. His home was almost destroyed. The television and desk in the living room were sitting where they had been before the storm, but the walls around them were gone. His parents and brothers had survived the storm in their storm cellar, but a family of four that had lived only a block away perished. A farmer in Idalou about seven miles away found his mother's driver's license. Six months after the tornado, area farmers continued to return his father's savings bonds they had found in their fields.

Because a tornado of such intensity rarely strikes a large city, especially high-rise buildings, many studied the Lubbock tornado. Sociologists studied the rebuilding patterns of the community and the role of the media in warning the Spanish-speaking citizens. Tornado expert Theodore Fujita of the University of Chicago mapped the storm's damage patterns in great detail. His analysis showed that the tornado seemingly "skipped around"; some buildings were completely destroyed while those next door or across the street were virtually untouched. From this information Fujita determined that the Lubbock tornado had been a multiple vortex one in which numerous small funnel clouds rotated around a larger central funnel. Fujita's studies of buildings in Lubbock that received various amounts of damage led to his development of the Fujita tornado intensity scale or F-scale. The Weather Bureau evaluated the preparedness of the city and concluded that the death toll might have reached five hundred if the citizens had not known what to do when the television and radio stations issued the warnings.

April 10, 1979: **Vernon (Wilbarger County)---F4**

Early in the day severe weather forecasters knew that tornadoes would threaten the Red River Valley of Oklahoma and Texas, but nothing appeared unusual to the residents of the area on the Tuesday before Easter. Just before 2 P.M. the National Severe Storms Forecast Center issued a tornado watch for north central Texas. Wichita Falls radio and television stations passed the information to the public, and storm spotters hurried to their designated observation posts. This routine is common in Texas during the spring. Very often no tornadoes form, but this was not the case on April 10. Three F2 and two F4 tornadoes roared through parts of six counties, leaving behind fifty-four dead, over eighteen hundred injured, and approximately $500 million in damages.

The narrow, weak tornado that sped across Foard County shortly after three that afternoon injured one but did little damage. Alerted by the tornado to their southwest, the Vernon police chief and the Wilbarger County sheriff dispatched patrol cars to watch the approaching storm. When it became evident that the thick, dark mass of clouds approaching Vernon was a tornado, they activated the warning sirens. In a few minutes' time the F4 twister passing through the southern and eastern parts of the town killed eleven and injured sixty-seven. The fierce winds mangled automobiles and blew tractor-trailer rigs off the highway. Eight of the deaths occurred in vehicles. The twister dissipated shortly after it crossed the Oklahoma border.

About thirty minutes after the Vernon tornado an F2 tornado killed a woman near Harrold (Wilbarger County). She had left her car and taken shelter under a tractor-trailer truck; the storm moved the truck, crushing her beneath its wheels. Another F2 twister damaged a few roofs in

Seymour. National Severe Storms Laboratory storm chasers photographed and documented the life cycle of this tornado.

April 2, 1982: **Paris (Lamar County)---F4**

The National Weather Service issued a tornado watch effective until noon for the Red River Valley of Texas, but no twisters touched down. Deteriorating conditions caused re-issuance of a tornado watch at 3 P.M. Within twenty minutes a supercell produced a tornado that destroyed six homes, two mobile homes, and took one life in the communities of Allen's Chapel and Allen's Point in neighboring Fannin County. No sooner had the emergency management coordinator for the city of Paris reached his office than amateur radio operators reported funnel clouds west of town. Emergency vehicles with sirens blaring patrolled the neighborhoods, warning of possible danger. At 4 o'clock one of the funnel clouds touched down in the northwest part of Paris and raced eastward across the city's north side, leaving behind 10 dead, 170 injured, and more than 1300 damaged or destroyed homes. Most residents of a mobile home park took shelter when they heard the warnings, but one family refused to leave--two members of the family died. Six others perished out in the open, and two died in their homes. Damages totaled more than $50 million. After leaving Paris, the tornado damaged more than one hundred buildings in Reno and Blossom, small towns just east of Paris.

A close-up view of the Paris tornado as it moved through town. From NWS.

November 15, 1987: **outbreak in Central and East Texas**

An outbreak of killer tornadoes that occurred unusually late in the year devastated parts of eleven central and east Texas counties. The nine F2 and F3 tornadoes claimed 10 lives and injured 186 on a Sunday afternoon. The first tornado of the day struck in late morning near Giddings (Lee County), leaving behind eighty-five damaged or destroyed homes and one severely injured person.

Shortly after noon two perished in a mobile home near Caldwell when a tornado cut a twelve-mile long path through rural parts of Burleson and Milam counties. Two hours later another tornado near Normangee in Leon County killed three of the four occupants of a mobile home. The costliest tornado of the day killed one, injured fifty-nine, and left behind $20 million in property damages when it struck Palestine and the surrounding area. Many

117

businesses along U.S. Highway 79 and two schools suffered heavy damage. City officials credited a ten-minute warning with saving numerous lives.

The day's deadliest tornado killed four and injured eighty-one when it cut a thirty-three-mile long path across parts of Cherokee and Smith counties. When KETK-TV meteorologist Mark Rowlett detected a large hook echo three miles south of Jacksonville at 3:48 P.M., he immediately ran to the control room to put a tornado warning on the air. The storm knocked the station off the air before he could finish—the area received no warning. Several communities northeast of Palestine suffered damages. A six-week-old child and a seventy-eight-year-old woman died in their mobile homes in Cherokee County; a mother and daughter died in their mobile home in Smith County. Damage estimates were $13 million. Four other tornadoes in surrounding counties injured twenty-one and left behind numerous destroyed homes and nearly thirty-four thousand dead chickens.

April 24, 2007: **Eagle Pass (Maverick County)—F3**

Although this tornado did not claim ten or more lives in the United States, the death toll from the tornado on both sides of the Rio Grande River was ten. Three perished in Piedras Negras, Mexico, and seven died in Texas.

The supercell that formed in Mexico produced a twister that struck Piedras Negras before it crossed the international border into Rosita Valley, a rural community southeast of Eagle Pass, about 7 PM. Ricardo Tijerina, like most residents of the area, expected a typical spring storm when they saw the clouds roll in. While it was on the ground for about four miles, the tornado destroyed an elementary school, 59 manufactured homes, and 57 houses and damaged numerous other buildings. More importantly, it claimed seven lives including five in one family whose mobile home was destroyed when the winds rolled it into the elementary school building; searchers found them huddle together in the remains of their home. Two others died when their house collapsed around them. The eighty-one who suffered minor injuries were treated at the Eagle Pass hospital. The border town of some 25,000 residents relied heavily on the Kickapoo tribe's Lucky Eagle Casino and trade with its cross-border neighbor for much of its economy. The casino suffered no damage. An investigation after the storm found that the two primary media outlets in the area had not sent out the NWS warning about the tornadoes. Neither Eagle Pass nor Piedras Negas has a siren warning system.

December 26, 2015: **Garland and Rowlett (Dallas/Rockwall Counties)—F4**

NOTE: This account is from my perspective. I live in Garland along George Bush Turnpike less than 5 miles from where the deaths and the heavy damage occurred. I huddled in the bathtub with a pillow over my head as this tornado came closer to my home. At one time a television meteorologist reported that the tornado was less than two blocks from my home, but fortunately, the information was wrong.

The twelve counties that comprise the Metroplex, the Dallas-Fort Worth metropolitan area, are home to seven million people. Although the area is no stranger to tornadoes, those that touch down are with few exceptions small, weak ones that damage roofs and knock down fences; occasionally they injure some residents and take a life. The 1957 Dallas tornado that killed 10 and the 2013 Johnson County twister that killed 7 were the deadliest storms to hit the Metroplex since record keeping began.

Although the SPC had begun warning days before that the day after Christmas would be a stormy one, very few people paid attention. Although I follow severe weather daily, I was not as concerned about the potential for deadly tornadoes as I usually am. The afternoon of the tornado my husband and I drove to our son's house across Lake Ray Hubbard from our home in Garland. On the way home we drove through the area that would soon be left in rubble. Writing about tornadoes is one thing but experiencing one first-hand and knowing exactly where the winds were tearing apart lives is another.

Darkness comes early in late December. The only way to see a tornado in the dark is when lightning flashes reveal the monsters. At 6 PM the Metroplex's first tornado touched down in the Glenn Heights area of Ellis County where it damaged several homes and a school. Just before this tornado, the local television stations took over all programming and instituted their "severe weather" mode; they all stay on the air continuously until all danger has cleared the Metroplex. That day was no different. As I flipped from one station to another, the meteorologists reported that the tornado had dissipated; I sighed in relief. Maybe the worst was over, but I was wrong.

At 6:45 a large tornado that developed at Sunnyvale began moving northward. In its path was Garland and Rowlett. Siren sounded throughout both cities, and the television meteorologist seemed to get more agitated as they realized that this was not the usual tornado that hit the Metroplex; this one was a large wedge-shaped tornado, and it was too dark outside for good observation. This monster moved into far southeastern Garland where it devastated the neighborhood just south of Interstate 30. Fortunately, with the adequate warning, no one died in this area although 127 homes were destroyed and 750 others received varying degrees of damage. Under cover of darkness, the monster cloud, at times up to 550 yards wide, continued its journey northeastward toward the intersection of the interstate and President George Bush Turnpike, less than a mile from the bridge that crosses Lake Ray Hubbard. Drivers were caught unaware. The horrific winds blew cars off the Interstate 30 onto the access road below. In the mangle of vehicles nine died. While on her way home from a hair salon, Petra Ruiz was talking on her phone to her husband when she screamed and his phone screen went black. She was a victim of the winds. LaShondra Whitaker had given her friend, Kimberly Tippett and Kimberly's one-year-old son Kamryn, a ride to East Texas that day. On the way home, they were in the wrong place at the wrong time. The tornado blew her vehicle off the road killing all three of the occupants. Seventy-seven-year-old Cecil Lowrie and his wife were returning home from dinner when the ferocious winds picked up their vehicle and threw it off a bridge; he died. Four others in vehicles died, bringing the death toll to nine.

The massive tornado kept churning. It crossed an arm of the lake before plowing head-on into a Rowlett neighborhood. There it damaged or destroyed 450 buildings. Seventy-three-year-old Trevor Heslop's home collapsed around him. He succumbed to his injuries eighteen days later. After devastating homes the tornado, now an F-3, kept on its northeast trajectory toward a busy commercial area that housed large grocery stores, medical offices, and a nursing home. In its path, the twister left behind incredible devastation to many of these buildings and more houses on the shore of Lake Ray Hubbard. Finally it dissipated over the lake. The total distance the F3/F4 tornado traveled was thirteen miles. In its path hundreds of homes were reduced to piles of rubble, and ten persons died. In true Texas spirit, everyone who was able jumped in to help. Some provided physical labor to clear piles of rubble while others gave money or needed goods to those in need. This tornado exemplifies how long a process recovery is. Cleanup is still going on four months after the deadly day. Blue tarps cover roofs, and some homes are being rebuilt, but it will take a long time to fully recover.

Vehicles were thrown from the I-30 bridge above to the access road in Garland. From NWS.

Damage in a Rowlett neighborhood. From NWS.

Chapter 7

Historically Important Texas Tornadoes

April 13, 1854: **Melrose (Nacogdoches County)**

One of the earliest recorded tornadoes in Texas destroyed much of the community of Melrose. The storm that meandered through the town in late afternoon destroyed several homes but took only one life. About twenty students were in class at the Union meeting house when the teacher, B.W. Brown, saw the storm approaching. He quickly tore up a board from the floor and placed the children under the building. Two boys ran out, and one was killed. Throughout the countryside fences and outbuildings crumbled in the path of the twister that ranged from one hundred yards to a mile wide.

May 28, 1854: **Gainesville (Cooke County)**

Another early Texas tornado struck the home of William Howeth west of Gainesville in Cooke County, killing five of the eight occupants. Late in the afternoon, Mrs. Howeth, her three children, and her husband's cousin Andy Howeth with his wife and two children took refuge from the roaring storm in the house. In a minute the house was destroyed, and Mr. Howeth and four children were killed. The body of one child was found four miles from the house. W. B. Parker who passed through the community more than a month after the storm wrote in his journal that the twister had blown a heavy ox-wagon several hundred yards and had deposited a horse and a sheep in the trees. Two years after the tornado Mrs. Albert Sydney Johnson passed through the community and was amazed at the amount of destruction that was still evident. She related that enormous trees were twisted and downed and that a horse was still lodged in a tree about ten feet above the ground.

May 15, 1949: **Amarillo (Potter County)**

Seven were killed and eighty-seven injured when a tornado cut across a south side residential area of Amarillo. About two hundred homes, many of them new ones occupied by World War II veterans, were damaged or destroyed; all of the deaths occurred in one block. The intense, narrow tornado derailed freight cars, damaged forty-five airplanes at the city's airport, and overturned tractor-trailer trucks. One of the trucks had been hauling pigs, and searchers found some the animals rooting through piles of debris that only minutes before had been new homes.

This tornado played a significant role in the creation of the Weather Bureau's forecasting system. At this time the Air Force issued tornado watches for military installations, but civilians received no comparable notices of impending severe weather. On the evening of the Amarillo tornado, military facilities in north Texas and southern Oklahoma were notified that tornadoes were possible, but the military had no authority to notify the Weather Bureau. When the tornado formed just west of the city, Amarillo Weather Bureau Chief Henry C. Winburn took an unprecedented step—at 8:17 P.M. he broke into radio broadcasts to warn residents to take cover. After the tornado, the *Amarillo Globe* severely criticized the Weather Bureau for not issuing a tornado forecast, and Senator Lyndon Johnson wanted to know why the Bureau was not doing more to forecast tornadoes. A lengthy controversy between the Air Force and the civilian severe weather forecasters followed until the Weather Bureau in 1952 agreed to issue tornado watches.

September 1, 1952: **Carswell Air Force Base (Tarrant County)----**not rated

The forecast for that Labor Day afternoon was for thunderstorms with winds of forty to sixty miles per hour. Shortly before six o'clock a thunderstorm rolled toward Carswell Air Force Base in Fort Worth. Snuggly tied down along the flight line were more than one hundred B-36 bombers which represented more than half of the Strategic Air Command's available striking force. Across the runways more than thirty of the massive bombers were parked on ramps at the manufacturing plant. Seconds after the thunderstorm struck the base, a tornado dropped from the clouds and flung the 139-ton planes like matchsticks. In a few minutes Mother Nature put the United States in a vulnerable military position—one B-36 was destroyed and seventy-one were damaged. Estimates of the damage ranged from $50 to $100 million.

This storm does not appear in any listing of tornadoes, but it was a significant event during the height of the Cold War. A Senate committee investigation criticized the Air Force for having so many of its bombers lined up wing to wing, just as susceptible to an enemy attack as the battleships lined up at Pearl Harbor were only eleven years earlier.

May 25, 1955: **Sterling County---**not rated

Tornadoes are threats not only to people and structures on the ground but also to aircraft. Airplanes usually do not fly through thunderstorms, especially ones strong enough to produce a tornado. Unfortunately, a B-36 bomber that flew into a tornado-producing thunderstorm about 10:50 P.M. crashed about sixty miles northwest of San Angelo, killing its fifteen crew members. The Air Force and Weather Bureau did not confirm a tornado was the cause of the crash, but the Sterling City sheriff said he saw a tornado while he was on the way to the crash site. Four of the bomber's ten jet engines were found about twenty-five miles from the remainder of the wreckage.

April 5, 1956: **Bryan (Brazos County)---F2**

When the Severe Local Storms Forecast Center issued a tornado watch for central Texas on April 5, 1956, meteorologists at Texas A&M began watching their radar scopes for signs of storms. At mid-afternoon a graduate student monitoring the radar saw a hook-echo associated with a storm rapidly approaching Bryan and College Station. He called his professor to take a look, and both agreed that the radar indicted a tornado was going to strike the twin cities. The professor notified the local police and radio station that a severe storm, possibly a tornado, would strike Bryan around three o'clock. Another professor warned the college authorities and the College Station School District of the approaching danger and urged them to keep all students in the classroom. The tornado struck Bryan at 3:10. Fortunately, authorities and citizens alike heeded the warning—no one was killed or injured. The remarkable aspect of the tornado was not the storm itself but that this was the first warning ever issued in the country based solely on radar observation.

April 3, 1964: **Wichita Falls (Wichita County)---F5**

A clear blue sky was overhead as many Wichita Falls residents who were downtown about 2:30 watched a tornado move across the city's northwest suburbs and

Sheppard Air Force Base. When a hook echo appeared on the Weather Bureau's radar screen, station KAUZ's cameras began a live scan of the skies. As the massive, spectacular twister roared through Sunset Terrace, Lincoln Heights, and Sheppard, the station rewarded its viewers with the first live television broadcast of a tornado. About ten minutes before the tornado struck, warning sirens had alerted the base to the approaching storm, and most of the fifteen thousand troops and civilian personnel took shelter. At the Sheppard School children huddled in the hallways as debris rained down around the building, but the twister did not strike the school. About three hundred students and instructors at the base's technical training facilities took refuge in a concrete hangar. Although the tornado heavily damaged the structure, no one inside was injured.

1964 Wichita Falls tornado. From NOAA Library

The F-5 tornado killed 7, injured 111, destroyed more than 225 homes, damaged 250 more, and left behind more than $15 million in damages. Only fifteen years later another tornado would strike the city; the statistics would be much grimmer.

September 20-21, 1967: **Southeast Texas**

Over the two-day period Hurricane Beulah spawned a record number of tornadoes across southeast Texas. Although various sources report from 47 to 141 tornadoes, the most comprehensive study lists 115 touchdowns.

The deadliest tornado struck near Palacios (Matagorda County) in the predawn hours, leaving behind three dead and seven injured. James Morgan, one of the injured, said the tornado blew him out the window and deposited him in a field across the highway from his home. Only a few feet away was the body of his grandmother who ironically had lived through a 1929 tornado at Bay City that claimed the lives of her two eldest sons. The only other reported death occurred in the Plainview community near El Campo (Wharton County). An elderly man died in the wreckage of one of the two homes the tornado destroyed. At least thirteen tornadoes swooped down on all sides of Houston. Fortunately, most tropically-formed tornadoes are relatively weak or the death toll would have been much greater than four.

May 6, 1973: **Valley Mills (McLennan County)---F5**

No one died or was injured when an F5 tornado obliterated two barns. Wind engineers gave the twister the highest Fujita rating because it carried a pickup truck half a mile.

April 29, 1976: **near Brownwood (Brown County)---F5**

A twin funnel tornado devastated a row of houses along the Lake Brownwood Dam highway about two miles north of Brownwood late in the afternoon. Many of the ten people injured in the storm reported they had been hurled hundreds of feet through the air. The tornado also tore through a row of hangars at the Brownwood Municipal Airport, scattering pieces of private airplanes for hundreds of yards. Fortunately, no one was killed in the tornado which the National Weather Service rated an F5.

May 17, 1989: **Jarrell (Williamson County)---F3**

Clocks in Jarrell stopped at 4:02 P.M. when a tornado plunged to earth during a driving rainstorm. Thirty-one were injured; most were occupants of the sixteen tractor-trailer trucks the tornado overturned on Interstate 35. In the town the twister heavily damaged or destroyed thirty-five homes, twelve mobile homes, and sixteen businesses. One woman died in the ruins of her mobile home. The Double File Trail Elementary School principal credited tornado drills and quick action by teachers and staff with diverting a disaster. About 450 kindergarten through fifth grade students knelt and covered their heads in the school's hallways while a tornado peeled off part of the roof and shattered windows. Practice on tornado drills had paid off--one minor injury occurred. Only eight years later a much deadly tornado would strike the tiny community.

November 21, 1992: **Channelview (Harris County)---F4**

Tornado outbreaks in late fall are uncommon, but in November 1992 conditions for the formation of numerous tornadoes in a short period of time were optimal. On the afternoon of November 21, tornadoes formed in southeast Texas, and during the next two days the storms spread eastward and northward. Ninety-four tornadoes killed 26, injured 641, and destroyed more than $291 million of property. This was the third largest outbreak of tornadoes in the United States to that date.

Fortunately, no fatalities occurred in Texas. One factor may have been the recently installed Doppler radar that allowed meteorologists at the Houston National Weather Service Office to issue warnings an average of twenty-five minutes before the twelve tornadoes that formed in their area of responsibility struck. Three weak tornadoes occurred in Wharton County between 1:30 and 2:45, and three more touched down in Fort Bend County after 2 P.M. The strongest of the Fort Bend tornadoes (F2) came to earth near Fulshear and moved into Harris County near Katy where it did considerable damage to West Side Airport.

About 3:30 the day's most devastating Texas twister roared into the Channelview area of Houston and quickly intensified to F4 strength. The tornado, at one point up to a mile wide, damaged more than twelve hundred buildings and injured fifteen. The National Weather Service survey team credited timely television warnings and an educated public for the absence of fatalities. Most Houstonians had been trained since third grade about actions to take to save their lives. A dramatic example of this knowledge involved five children left at home when the mother went shopping. When the oldest realized a tornado was headed toward their house, he put three siblings under the bed while he and the other child hid in the closet. All escaped injury although the tornado heavily damaged the home.

About the same time of the Channelview tornado an F2 tornado touched down on the edge of Hermann Park and moved northeast across several highways, leaving in its wake six injured and more than six hundred buildings damaged. Before moving eastward into Louisiana, the storm system generated three tornadoes in Liberty County and one in Polk County.

April 25, 1994: **De Soto/Lancaster (Dallas County)---F4**

Heavily-populated southern Dallas County could have sustained heavy loss of life when an F4 tornado ravaged parts of De Soto and Lancaster under cover of darkness. Although three died and fifty-five were injured, officials credited the brand new Doppler radar located in Fort Worth with saving many more lives. The Doppler enable meteorologists to give a few minutes' warning of the approaching storm, time that enabled the two towns to active their warning sirens. Many escaped injury by taking cover in bathrooms and closets. The tornado destroyed or heavily damaged more than two hundred homes and fifty-eight businesses in Lancaster and seventy-five homes and ten businesses in De Soto. Damages totaled more than $200 million.

Much of Lancaster's historic Town Square lay in ruins. One city council member told the *Dallas Morning News* that "it absolutely took the heart out of Lancaster. I don't know how you can rebuild 100 years of history." All of the deaths occurred in a residential area near the square.

One of the victims, Rable Cobb, had written the town's history including drawings of many of the old homes.

In DeSoto the twister demolished the southern end of the new civic center. Inside the center's gymnasium two of the thirty-seven people who huddled in a restroom received minor injuries. A woman caught in her car when the storm struck was severely injured when the tornado blew her Toyota one hundred yards across the center's parking lot and into a second-floor window of the building.

Historically, this tornado is important, not because of the lives it claimed or the damage it left behind, but because of the lives that were saved. After the storm local, state, and national media focused on the Doppler radar that had provided television stations and local officials enough time to warn citizens to take actions to safeguard their lives.

June 2 and June 8, 1995: **Pampa (Gray County)---F4**

Ten significant and numerous smaller tornadoes swarmed across the Texas Panhandle during this historic week. Although none took a life and only three caused injury, these tornadoes are notable because they are some of the most studied thus far. During the spring of 1994 and 1995 the National Severe Storms Laboratory and the Center for Analysis and Prediction of Storms conducted a joint large-scale tornado observation program called VORTEX. In June 1995 the team deployed vehicles equipped with mobile Doppler radar, multiple video cameras, and the latest meteorological instruments to accumulate data from storms in an effort to determine what triggered tornado formation. Their efforts were rewarded on June 2 when they observed an F3 tornado that moved across the southern edge of Friona (Parmer County). The multiple-vortex tornado injured twelve and destroyed or damaged forty homes and twenty-five businesses including the town's largest employer, the Hi-Pro Feed Mill. When the VORTEX field coordinator spotted another storm developing to the southeast, he sent the armada to Castro County. As more than one hundred scientists and storm chasers watched, a tornado formed about four miles southeast of Dimmitt and moved to the northeast for six miles, leaving behind a few damaged buildings and no injuries. Along Highway 86 the twister sucked up several hundred feet of black top. For the first time in history, the internal structure of a tornado was observed on a radar screen. Meteorologists collected massive quantities of data, hundreds of photos, and substantial videotape footage of this tornado.

Six days later (June 8) the VORTEX armada was rewarded with an outbreak of seven tornadoes in the Panhandle. The most spectacular and extensively photographed twister of the day moved slowly from three

Two views of the Dimmitt tornado from Project VORTEX. From NOAA photo library.

miles southwest of Pampa (Gray County) to the edge of the city. The $30 million in losses included more than one hundred homes and fifty businesses destroyed or heavily damaged. Winds estimated at more than two hundred miles per hour injured seven. This Pampa supercell produced at least eight more tornadoes, but non inflicted injury or did much damage.

A second family of tornadoes that swarmed across Donley, Gray, Wheeler, and Hemphill counties on June 8 left no humans injured and about $15 million in damages. The two F4 tornadoes that struck Wheeler County killed more than eight hundred head of livestock including several hundred head of cattle at the Wheeler Stockyard.

March 28, 2000: Fort Worth (Tarrant County)---F3

Fort Worth was the only major American city in "tornado country" without a recorded tornado death. Maybe it was "dumb luck," or perhaps it was the American Indian belief that tornadoes would not strike where two rivers converged (two forks of the Trinity River merge at Fort Worth) that had protected Cowtown for more than 150 years. Luck ran out shortly after 6 P.M. when a destructive tornado tore through residential areas and downtown.

Sirens sounded a few minutes before the tornado touched down in a residential area four miles west of downtown. Moving along Seventh Street, the twister struck the Montgomery Ward building and numerous small businesses, then nearly destroyed the Cash America building. The tornado weakened as it entered downtown, but the flying debris broke thousands of windows. Office furniture, computers, and plates of glass plummeted to the ground, but fortunately no one was seriously injured. The twister left behind two dead and eighty injured, but Fort Worth was lucky. Only a year before experts had predicted that a head-on strike on the downtown area could kill three hundred and cost $2.6 billion.

The Fort Worth tornado dissipated east of downtown, but the thunderstorm spawned a new twister in Arlington about 7 P.M. This F3 tornado cut a five-mile long path through residential areas before moving into Grand Prairie. No deaths or serious injuries occurred, but unusual incidents did. In one home a telephone and answering machine disappeared from a nightstand, but seventy-five cents lying beside them remained untouched. At another house the storage shed disappeared but another appeared in its place.

The two tornadoes destroyed more than one hundred homes and damaged nearly one thousand others including the one-time residence of Lee Harvey Oswald. Damages were in excess of $450 million, making this one of the costliest storms in Texas history.

December 29, 2006: **outbreak in Central and East Texas**

Two unusual events occurred on December 29, 2006: the largest winter outbreak of tornadoes in recorded Texas history struck the state, and the President and First Lady of the United States had to take shelter as tornadoes danced around the area of their Central Texas ranch. Twenty-six tornadoes swarmed across the state; twenty-two of them occurred in the Fort Worth/Dallas Weather Forecast Office's warning area. Several of the twisters carved long paths through twelve north Texas counties taking one life, injuring thirty, and leaving behind millions of dollars of damage. The first tornado of the outbreak touched down three miles southwest of Oglesby (Coryell County) about 1:30 P.M., and the last appeared near Palestine (Anderson County) at 7:30 P.M. An F2 tornado in Limestone County struck a retirement home for veterans four miles southwest of Groesbeck; one elderly man died and several sustained injuries. The costliest storm of the day left behind $2.8 million in damages in College Station (Brazos County).

President George W. Bush and his wife Laura were visiting their Crawford ranch (McLennan County) when tornado warnings were issued for the area. The Secret Service moved the President and First Lady into an armored vehicle and drove the couple to a tornado shelter on their ranch, but they never had to enter the shelter as the storm moved by without dropping a tornado.

The 20 Deadliest US Tornadoes

RANK	LOCATION	DATE	DEATHS
1	Tri-State (MO, IL, IN)	March 18, 1925	695
2	Natchez, MS	May 6, 1840	317
3	St. Louis, MO	May 27, 1896	255
4	Tupelo, MS	April 5, 1936	216
5	Gainesville, GA	April 6, 1936	203
6	Woodward, OK & Higgins, TX	April 9, 1947	181
7	Joplin, MO	May 22, 2011	151
8	Amite, LA & Purvis, MS	April 24, 1908	143
9	New Richmond, WI	June 12, 1899	117
10	Flint, MI	June 8, 1953	115
11t	Waco, TX	May 11, 1953	114
11t	Goliad, TX	May 18, 1902	114
13	Omaha, NE	March 23, 1913	103
14	Mattoon, IL	May 26, 1917	101
15	Shinnston, WV	June 23, 1944	100
16	Marshfield, MO	April 18, 1880	99
17	Gainesville & Holland, GA	June 1, 1903	98
18	Poplar Bluff, MO	May 9, 1927	98
19	Snyder, OK	May 10, 1905	97
20	Natchez, MS	April 24, 1908	91

Tornadoes and Deaths by County 1950-2020

COUNTY	TORNADOES	DEATHS
Anderson	34	2
Andrews	25	0
Angelina	42	2
Aransas	13	0
Archer	27	0
Armstrong	43	0
Atascosa	16	0
Austin	26	0
Bailey	54	0
Bandera	7	0
Bastrop	32	0
Baylor	25	0
Bee	34	0
Bell	63	3
Bexar	70	3
Blanco	18	0
Borden	11	0
Bosque	38	2
Bowie	53	2
Brazoria	92	0
Brazos	28	0
Brewster	20	0
Briscoe	46	25
Brooks	5	0

Brown	38	0
Burleson	20	2
Burnet	32	0
Caldwell	23	0
Calhoun	30	0
Callahan	47	5
Cameron	62	0
Camp	12	0
Carson	88	0
Cass	61	0
Castro	66	3
Chambers	31	4
Cherokee	39	3
Childress	26	0
Clay	33	0
Cochran	30	0
Coke	14	0
Coleman	41	2
Collin	45	2
Collingsworth	42	0
Colorado	32	1
Comal	13	0
Comanche	39	0
Concho	28	0
Cooke	57	0
Coryell	34	0
Cottle	35	1
Crane	20	0
Crockett	10	0
Crosby	57	1
Culberson	6	0
Dallam	31	0
Dallas	102	13
Dawson	50	0
Deaf Smith	38	0

Delta	7	2
Denton	53	0
Dewitt	15	0
Dickens	40	0
Dimmitt	3	0
Donley	60	16
Duval	18	0
Eastland	53	1
Ector	44	0
Edwards	3	0
El Paso	6	0
Ellis	54	0
Erath	44	0
Falls	14	0
Fannin	53	1
Fayette	31	0
Fisher	49	0
Floyd	57	1
Foard	20	0
Fort Bend	57	1
Franklin	14	0
Freestone	12	0
Frio	14	5
Gaines	36	0
Galveston	122	9
Garza	20	0
Gillespie	17	0
Glasscock	24	0
Goliad	20	0
Gonzales	21	0
Gray	80	2
Grayson	70	2
Gregg	36	0
Grimes	13	0
Guadalupe	23	0

Hale	129	8
Hall	52	1
Hamilton	25	0
Hansford	66	0
Hardeman	36	0
Hardin	26	1
Harris	241	12
Harrison	77	0
Hartley	36	0
Haskell	55	13
Hays	29	1
Hemphill	48	1
Henderson	34	0
Hidalgo	40	0
Hill	52	13
Hockley	61	0
Hood	28	6
Hopkins	31	0
Houston	29	1
Howard	54	0
Hudspeth	11	0
Hunt	60	0
Hutchinson	72	1
Irion	14	0
Jack	23	0
Jackson	42	0
Jasper	57	3
Jeff Davis	11	0
Jefferson	104	3
Jim Hogg	4	0
Jim Wells	44	0
Johnson	102	0
Jones	83	1
Karnes	22	0
Kaufman	37	1

Kendall	20	0
Kenedy	6	0
Kent	24	0
Kerr	11	0
Kimble	7	0
King	21	0
Kinney	13	0
Kleberg	30	0
Knox	25	5
La Salle	1	0
Lamar	40	11
Lamb	85	0
Lampasas	15	0
Lavaca	35	0
Lee	27	0
Leon	21	0
Liberty	63	0
Limestone	24	1
Lipscomb	40	0
Live Oak	33	0
Llano	11	0
Loving	7	0
Lubbock	95	26
Lynn	45	0
Madison	15	3
Marion	20	0
Martin	37	0
Mason	12	1
Matagorda	47	4
Maverick	13	0
McCulloch	28	0
McLennan	60	114
McMullen	6	0
Medina	26	3
Menard	2	0

Midland	33	0
Milam	22	1
Mills	12	0
Mitchell	55	0
Montague	48	1
Montgomery	49	0
Moore	57	0
Morris	13	0
Motley	23	0
Nacogdoches	49	3
Navarro	46	1
Newton	31	0
Nolan	49	1
Nueces	106	2
Ochiltree	59	2
Oldham	24	0
Orange	27	1
Palo Pinto	40	0
Panola	42	0
Parker	66	0
Parmer	50	1
Pecos	82	2
Polk	29	0
Potter	38	0
Presidio	5	0
Rains	14	1
Randall	78	1
Reagan	16	0
Real	2	0
Red River	32	0
Reeves	47	30
Refugio	25	0
Roberts	32	0
Robertson	14	0
Rockwall	16	0

Runnels	52	0
Rusk	52	0
Sabine	18	1
San Augustine	20	0
San Jacinto	19	1
San Patricio	56	0
San Saba	17	0
Schleicher	11	0
Scurry	38	0
Shackelford	25	0
Shelby	38	3
Sherman	39	0
Smith	67	2
Somervell	6	0
Starr	4	0
Stephens	22	0
Sterling	17	0
Stonewall	26	0
Sutton	5	0
Swisher	71	4
Tarrant	101	3
Taylor	68	1
Terrell	7	0
Terry	36	0
Throckmorton	42	3
Titus	26	2
Tom Green	53	15
Travis	68	2
Trinity	24	0
Tyler	21	0
Upshur	23	0
Upton	19	0
Uvalde	14	0
Val Verde	42	0
Van Zandt	41	2

Victoria	38	0
Walker	17	1
Waller	18	1
Ward	16	0
Washington	26	4
Webb	10	0
Wharton	68	1
Wheeler	54	1
Wichita	61	51
Wilbarger	52	14
Willacy	20	0
Williamson	67	29
Wilson	18	0
Winkler	11	0
Wise	59	2
Wood	45	0
Yoakum	25	0
Young	52	2
Zapata	5	0
Zavala	9	0

Texas Tornado Deaths by Decade

This data is from Grazulis

1880's	48
1890's	179
1900's	299
1910's	122
1920's	232
1930's	188
1940's	172

This data is from the NCDC data base

1950's	214
1960's	37
1970's	139
1980's	76
1990's	50
2000's	22
2010's	35

Tornadoes and Schools

LOCATION	COUNTY	DATE	THE EVENT
Milano Junction	Milam	April 27, 1883	9 students badly injured at McGregor's schoolhouse
Prairie Grove	Limestone	April 22, 1885	A 14-year-old girl and 18 injuries at the destroyed school
Brookston	Lamar	May 23, 1888	80 children fled the school before it was destroyed
Forestburg	Montague	May 17, 1889	2 children killed
Austin	Travis	March 28, 1897	Brackenridge Hall, a dormitory at University of Texas, unroofed
Itasca	Hill	March 11, 1902	2 teachers and 2 students injured at Rockwall

			School during lunch hour
Holliday	Archer	May 5, 1904	teacher died and 1 student injured when school building picked up and dropped on its roof; other students had fled for shelter at the sight of the funnel
Briggs	Burnet	April 12, 1906	8 children and the principal were injured when walls crashed on them
Melissa	Collin	April 13, 1921	240 children huddled under desks while upper level of the building was blown away; a teacher and 3 children injured
Austin	Travis	May 4, 1922	1 student killed at a St.

			Edwards University dorm
Atlanta	Cass	April 13, 1927	A boy's finger was cut off by flying glass at a school
Slocum	Anderson	April 24,1929	Struck at school lunch hour; students ran to end of building and lay down between desks; 1 student killed and a dozen more injured as school blew apart
Shelbyville	Shelby	March 30, 1933	25 students and a teacher injured at Calgary School
Laird Hill	Rusk	May 10, 1943	103 students in Laird Hill school when tornado blew it apart; all were injured, 2 teachers and 10 students

			seriously
McKinney	Collin	May 3, 1948	A few 4, 5, and 6 grade students were injured and a teacher lost a finger when their school was unroofed; no high school students were injured when the tornado blew in a wall
Olney	Young	May 18, 1951	A few students were injured by flying glass as they hid under desks
San Angelo	Tom Green	May 11, 1953	The roof and several walls collapsed while students were in hallways; a dozen had minor injuries
Beulah	Angelina	April 30,	When

		1954	students noticed tree-tops were snapping in a storm, they hid under desks; 2 teachers and 2 students were hospitalized when the rural school partially collapsed
Tyler	Rusk	April 26, 1957	3 elementary school students who arrived at school early were injured; auditorium at Tyler Junior College badly damaged
Lacoste School	Medina	May 2, 1958	Students huddled in first floor hallway when school was unroofed; one student injured
Bay Ridge	Fort Bend	April 19,	1 student

Christian		1965	killed and 3 injured when a tornado badly damaged a dormitory and unroofed a shop building at Bay Ridge Christian College
Miami	Roberts	May 6, 1968	200 students at Miami High School were taken to basement for safety; tornado destroyed the school; 4 students injured when they didn't remain in the basement
Whiteface	Cochran	April 17, 1970	5 people injured attending a senior play in the school auditorium
DeSoto	Dallas	May 3, 1979	A few students suffered minor

			injuries when they were sheltered in lower interior hallways; roof, windows, doors, and many automobiles in the school parking lot damaged
DeSoto	Dallas	May 13, 1985	Several students at Lake June School injured by flying glass; junior high school in De Soto heavily damaged
Marble Falls	Burnet	May 13, 1994	High school damaged while students had taken shelter; a preschool day care center damaged but no children injured
League City	Galveston	February	Tornado

		10, 1998	touched down at Clear Creek High School; windows blown out; 4 injuries from flying glass
DeKalb	Bowie	May 4, 1999	High school suffered severe damage; no one injured because siren had sounded 15 minutes before tornado
Corpus Christi	Nueces	October 24, 2002	1 fatality and 14 injuries at Del Mar College
Tuscola	Taylor	March 4, 2004	Two injured at Jim Ned High School
Forney		April 3, 2012	Vehicles in parking lot and roof damage to Crosby Elementary School; no students injured; principal helped

			students find shelter; building shook; no students injured at North Forney High School when school sustained damage while classes were in session

Sources

Government Documents

U. S. Department of Agriculture. Weather Bureau. *Report on the Tornadoes of May 12 and 15, 1896* by Isaac Cline. Galveston, 1896.

U. S. Department of Commerce. National Oceanic and Atmospheric Administration. National Climatic Data Center. *Storm Events.* Asheville, N.C., 2013.

U. S. Department of Commerce. Environmental Science Services Administration. National Weather Service. *The Lubbock, Texas, Tornado, May 11, 1970.* Rockville, Maryland, 1970.

U. S. Department of Commerce. National Oceanic and Atmospheric Administration. National Weather Service. *The Central Texas Tornadoes of May 27, 1997.* Silver Spring, Maryland, 1998.

_____. *The Desoto/Lancaster Tornado, April 25, 1994.* Fort Worth, Texas, 1994.

_____. *Red River Valley Tornadoes of April 10, 1979.* Rockville, Maryland, 1980.

_____. *The Saragosa, Texas, Tornado, May 22, 1987.* Fort Worth, Texas, 1988.

_____. *The Widespread November 21-23, 1992, Tornado Outbreak: Houston to Raleigh and Gulf Coast to Ohio Valley.* Silver Spring, Maryland, 1993.

____. *Overview and Analysis of the 29 December 2006 Texas Tornado Outbreak* by Gregory R. Patrick et al. Fort Worth, Texas, 2009.

Books and Articles

Aguirre, Benigno et al. *Saragosa, Texas, Tornado May 22, 1987*: *An Evaluation of the Warning System.* Washington, D.C.: National Academy Press, 1991.

Bedard, Richard. *In the Shadow of the Tornado.* Norman, Oklahoma: Gilco Publishing, 1996.

Bonham Public Library. *Fannin County Folks and Facts.* Dallas: Taylor Publishing Co., 1977.

Bradford, Marlene. *Scanning the Skies: A History of Tornado Forecasting.* Norman: University of Oklahoma Press, 2001.

Briscoe County Historical Survey Committee. *Footprints in Time in Briscoe County 1876-1976.* Silverton, Texas: Briscoe County Historical Committee,1976.

Chrisman, Brutus Clay. *Early Days in Callahan County.* Self-published, 1966.

Fenoglio, Melvin. E. *Looking Back: Moments in Montague County History.* Montague, Texas: Aurelia Press, 1999.

"Frost Tornado." Navarro County Texas Genealogical and Historical Website. Available at www.rootsweb.com/~txnavarr.

Grazulis, Thomas P. *Significant Tornadoes, 1680-1991.* St. Johnsbury, Vermont: Environmental Films, 1993.

Harris, Jay et al, eds. *The Wichita Falls, Vernon, and Lawton Tornadoes*.
C. F. Boone, 1979.

"How A Tornado Crippled the B-36 Fleet," *Aviation Week*, February 2, 1953.

Knox County History Committee. *Knox County History*. Haskell, Texas:
Haskell Free Press, 1966.

Lane, Derwood. *Saragosa: The Town Killed by a Tornado*. Austin: Eakins
Press, 1989.

Mahaney, Chip. "April 2, 1957: Dallas' Date with Disaster," *Storm Track*,
May/June 1997.

"Melrose, Texas, Destruction of Life and Property, April 1854."Available at
www3.gendisasters.com/texas/5828/Melrose-tx-destruction-life-property-apr-1854.

Paris News. *Tornado: Paris, Texas, April 2, 1982*. Paris: The Paris News, 1982.

Piner, H. L. *Sherman's Black Friday: A History of the Great Sherman Tornado*. Sherman, Texas: Register Printing House, 1896.

"SAC Crippled," *Aviation Week*, September 22, 1952.

Smith, W. Morton. *The First 100 Years in Cooke County*. San Antonio: Naylor Co., 1955.

Taylor, William Charles. *A History of Clay County*. Austin: Jenkins Publishing
Co., 1972.

Turner, Hicks A., ed. *I Remember Callahan: History of Callahan County*. Dallas: Taylor Publishing Co., 1986.

Weems, John. *The Tornado*. College Station, Texas: Texas A&M University Press, 1977.

Zephyr Mirror. *One of Life's Greatest Tragedies: A True and Comprehensive History of the Zephyr Cyclone, May 29, 1909.* Zephyr, Texas: Zephyr Mirror, 1909.

Newspapers

Austin Statesman
Bonham News
Brownwood Bulletin
Bryan Daily Eagle
Dallas Morning News
Dallas Times Herald
Fort Worth Star-Telegram
Houston Chronicle
Houston Post
Houston Post-Dispatch
Lubbock Avalanche Journal
McKinney Express
New York Times
Odessa American
Pecos Enterprise
San Antonio Express
Sherman Courier
Sherman Daily Democrat
Victoria Weekly Advocate
Waco News Tribune
Wichita Falls Times

Personal letters in possession of author:

Boren, C. K., May 2000.
Meissner, Allen, May 1998.
Peterson,   LaDonna,   October   1998.

About the Author

Marlene Bradford has spent most of her life in Tornado Alley. When living in Lawrence, Kansas, Joe Eagleman, a meteorology professor at the University of Kansas, encouraged her to write tornado history. Her doctoral dissertation at Texas A&M University was the story of the tornado watch and warning system which was published under the title *Scanning the Skies: A History of Tornado Forecasting*. She is also the author of *Arkansas Tornadoes: The Natural State's Deadliest Twisters* and *Incredible Destruction in Central Texas: The Jarrell Tornado* as well as the editor of *Notable Natural Disasters*. Her love (besides tornadoes) is teaching. The author has recently retired from more than twenty years of teaching U.S. history at the college and high school level and currently resides with her husband in Garland, Texas.